The Testamentum Domini:

A Text for Students, with Introduction, Translation, and Notes

by Grant Sperry-White

THE ALCUIN CLUB and the GROUP FOR RENEWAL OF WORSHIP (GROW)

The Alcuin Club, which exists to promote the study of Christian liturgy in general and of Anglican liturgy in particular, traditionally published a single volume annually for its members. This ceased in 1986. Similarly, GROW was responsible from 1975 to 1986 for the quarterly 'Grove Liturgical Studies'. Since the beginning of 1987 the two have sponsored a Joint Editorial Board to produce quarterly 'Joint Liturgical Studies'. Both also produce separate publications and details are available from both separately.

THE COVER PICTURE

shows a page from Rahmani's edition of the *Testamentum* overlaying the title page of the *Testamentum* from Vööbus' edition, taken from the *Synodicon*

First Impression September 1991
ISSN 0951-2667
ISBN 1 85174 189 5

 GROVE BOOKS LIMITED
Bramcote   Nottingham   NG9 3DS

CONTENTS

CHAPTER

PAGE

Introduction 5

1. Eucharist (I. 23, 24, 35; II.10) 13

2. Christian Initiation (II.5-10) 23

3. Daily Prayer (I.22, 26, 32, 42, 43; II.24) 31

4. Ordination (I.21, 30, 38, 41, 44, 45) 40

5. Architecture (I.19) 46

6. Liturgical Year (II.12, 18, 19, 20) 48

Preface

Some of the translations appearing in this volume were produced during a year's study under the direction of Dr. Sebastian Brock of the Oriental Institute of Oxford University. I wish to express my gratitude to the British Fulbright Commission for its generous support without which the majority of this work could not have been done. I wish to thank Dr. Brock for his patient tutelage in the areas of Syriac and Greek translation and patrology; the responsibility for any errors is, of course, mine. I wish also to thank the Rev. Canon Dr. Paul F. Bradshaw for recommending the *Testamentum* for inclusion in the Alcuin/GROW series. Finally, a special note of thanks to my wife Beth for her constant support and encouragement.

The Editor

Grant Sperry-White is a doctoral candidate in the Department of Theology, University of Notre Dame, Indiana, U.S.A.

Introduction

I. THE TESTAMENTUM DOMINI

The *Testamentum Domini* (hereafter **T**) is a church order composed originally in Greek which survives today in Syriac, Ethiopic and Arabic (with possible fragments in Greek and Coptic) as books one and two of the canonical collection known as the Clementine Octateuch. Its directions are cast in the form of Jesus' instructions to his disciples, an 'ecclesiastical rule' (I.17), during the time between the resurrection and ascension. As this literary device is only nominally followed in the body of the text, we can speak of the *Testamentum* primarily as a church order preceded by an apocalypse. The two books of the Syriac text are composed of 74 chapters of varying length:

Introduction: I.1-3
Apocalypse: I. 4-13
Transition: I.14-18
Church Order: I.19-II.25
Conclusion: II.26-27

The *Testamentum* had been known to Western scholars since the sixteenth century, but portions of the text were not edited until the mid-nineteenth century. The first complete edition of the Syriac text appeared in 1899 under the editorship of the Syrian Patriarch Ignatius Ephrem II Rahmani.[1] Although Ludolf published the Ethiopic Anaphora of Our Lord in the seventeenth century[2], the full Ethiopic text was not edited in its entirety until 1984 (see below for a discussion of this edition).[3] The Arabic remains unedited, except for Baumstark's edition of the initiation and eucharistic rites.[4]

Rahmani's edition appeared on the scene during a period of intense scholarly interest in the ancient church orders. For a time, many church historians and patrologists produced studies on the *Testamentum*. Many of these monographs attempted to assign the *Testamentum* its proper place among the other ancient church orders which had come to light in the previous thirty years. Some saw the *Testamentum* as the source of other church orders, including the Canons of Hippolytus, Apostolic Constitutions VIII and the document which would eventually be known as the Apostolic Tradition (hereafter **ApTrad**). With Connolly's and Schwarz's independent discovery that **ApTrad** itself was the source of many of the other church orders, interest in the *Testamentum* faded. Since the first decade of the twentieth century, no scholar has devoted an entire monograph to the *Testamentum* (apart from Beylot's edition of the Ethiopic). The document has acquired a slightly negative reputation as a 'rehash' (to use the phrase of J.N.D.

---

[1] No. 13 in the Bibliography.
[2] No. 10 in the Bibliography.
[3] No. 2 in the Bibliography.
[4] No. 1 in the Bibliography.

Kelly) of **ApTrad**, the 'last gasp' of the church order *genre* produced by a group on the fringes of ecclesial life. This characterization is undeserved.

II. DATE

When speaking of the 'date' of **T**, we refer to the date of the final compilation of the document, apart from the issue of the age of the individual components which **T** comprises.

Rahmani suggested that the *Testamentum* belonged to the second century. Few others have followed his lead. Drews suggested a mid- to late-fourth century date, while Harnack and Baumstark proposed the fifth to the sixth century. Maclean settled upon a mid-fourth century dating, while Russian scholars have tended to follow Rahmani. Today, many if not most authors accept Harnack's fifth century date for the document.

The question of the document's date is still open. Those who argue for a late date base their arguments, in general, upon post-Constantinopolitan theological terminology and the supposed existence of the office of archdeacon. However, as Maclean has shown, the office of archdeacon does not appear in **T**, and one major witness to the **T** text (the Ethiopic) does not contain the advanced theological terminology the Syriac version contains (cf. 1.41). The internal evidence, therefore, supports a date sometime in the second half of the fourth century, probably before 381.

III. PLACE OF ORIGIN

Syria, Asia Minor and Egypt have all been proposed as the document's place of origin. 'Syria' seems too broad a geographical category to be of much use; the liturgical materials of the *Testamentum* do not bear any special resemblance to those described by fourth century Syrian writers. There are a few correspondences between the *Testamentum* and the Canons of Hippolytus, written in Egypt between 336 and 340.

A number of factors speak in favour of Asia Minor. 1. The horarium the document describes bears some resemblance to that of the so-called 'urban monastic' office of Basil and others. 2. The *Testamentum* has many parallels with a late fourth century Cappadocian document, the pseudo-Athanasian *De virginitate*. 3. The widows have a prominent place in the document, including the right of gathering with the other clergy at the altar at the celebration of the eucharist.

IV. AUTHORSHIP

The question of authorship is one of the most disputed of all the questions surrounding the *Testamentum*. The traditional view is that the document was produced by a 'fringe' community clearly outside the mainstream of ecclesial life. This interpretation is not entirely tenable today, given what we know of the diversity of ecclesial life in the fourth century. The fact that **T** was included in the Clementine Octateuch suggests that it had support in the circles that produced the Octateuch, support it might well have lacked had it been the product of a heterodox community.

The extreme anti-Arian theological terminology the document contains suggests that **T** emerged from anti-Arian circles, perhaps prior to the Council of Constantinople in 381. Some have suggested that **T** should be ascribed to Apollinaris of Laodicea or his circle, but no indisputable evidence links **T** directly to Apollinaris.[1] While no certain identification of **T**'s author or authors is yet possible, it is not implausible to suggest that **T** was produced in extreme anti-Arian circles which were in contact with ascetic communities of Cappadocia. See the introduction to the **T** daily prayer texts below.

V. SOURCES

We can identify at least three sources for the *Testamentum*: the so-called Apostolic Tradition, an apocalypse which once circulated independently, and the practice of an unknown community, perhaps that which produced the *Testamentum*.

1. Apostolic Tradition, in some form. **T** differs from the other church orders which utilize **ApTrad** as a source, Apostolic Constitutions VIII and the Canons of Hippolytus, in that it shows great 'respect' for its source. Often, **T** does not alter the wording or sequence of its source, but merely adds blocs of material to the **ApTrad** text.[2] Because of this attitude toward **ApTrad** as a source, historians of the text of **ApTrad** (particularly Dix) have relied upon **T** to provide a relatively 'pure' text, as opposed to other witnesses to the text of **ApTrad**.

2. An apocalypse which circulated independently.[3]

3. The practice of an unknown community. This last 'source' is, obviously, the most difficult to document. However, when one separates the first two sources from the text of **T**, much of what is left often is relatively homogeneous in phraseology and terminology.

VI. INTEGRITY OF THE TEXT

As of this date, no satisfactory critical edition of any version of **T** exists. Rahmani's edition took into account all the manuscripts he knew, but in no way can his work be called a critical edition. The Ethiopic text edited by Beylot contains an critical apparatus, but there are problems with both the apparatus and the translation. After taking a number of random samplings of Beylot's Ethiopic text and its critical apparatus, the late Roger Cowley in his review of Beylot's edition wrote:

'Dr. Beylot is to be thanked for stimulating further study of the TD, but it must be concluded that his edition is insufficiently precise to be used for settling questions such as the existence of recensions of the Ethiopic text, its (or their) relationship to the Syriac and Arabic versions, and the possibility of a Greek original.'[4]

As was mentioned above, the Arabic remains unedited.

---

[1] See below in the section on Initiation for a phrase in the baptismal creed which some have linked to Apollinaris.
[2] E.g., the anaphora (I.23) and the bishop's ordination prayer (I.21).
[3] For more information, see no. 17 in the Bibliography.
[4] Cowley, Bibliography No. 2, p.295.

At this time, we cannot be sure of the wording of the Greek text or texts which lay behind the Syriac and (perhaps) Ethiopic. To date, only Baumstark and Coquin have addressed the problem of the relation of the different language versions to each other.[1] In 1974 René-Georges Coquin took some preliminary soundings of the Syriac, Ethiopic and Copto-Arabic translations, and produced a provisional stemma of the known versions of **T**. Coquin concluded that at least some of the Ethiopic translations of **T** were made directly from the Greek.[2]

VII. PREVIOUS EDITIONS (numbers refer to the Bibliography)

According to a colophon in the Syriac MSS M and B, the *Testamentum* was translated from the Greek into Syriac by one 'James the poor' in the year '998 of the Greeks', or A.D. 687. This James is probably to be identified with the Syrian Monophysite scholar and translator James of Edessa.[3]

1. Lagarde (Bib. Nos. 8, 9): A selection from Codex Sangermanensis 38 (**S**) which contains extracts from the entire *Testamentum*. Bib. No. 9 contains Lagarde's retroversion of **S** into Greek. The Syriac was utilized by Rahmani in his edition.

2. Rahmani (Bib. No. 13): A text utilizing three Syriac MSS: **M, B**, and **S** (see Abbreviations for further information).

3. Vööbus (Bib. No. 15): The West Syrian Synodicon, from a single Syriac MS (see Abbreviations under SYN for more information).

VIII. TRANSLATIONS INTO MODERN LANGUAGES

The Syriac has been translated into English and French. The Ethiopic has been translated into French. The Arabic has not been translated into any modern language.

ENGLISH: In 1902 James Cooper and Arthur John Maclean published an English translation of Rahmani's text with introduction and notes, entitled *The Testament of Our Lord* (T.& T. Clark, Edinburgh, 1902). The translation is literal, and its phraseology is that of formal, almost liturgical, English. Cooper and Maclean's notes are extensive, and some remain useful today if used with caution. However, their notes contain little commentary on the liturgical materials of the *Testamentum*.

In 1975 Arthur Vööbus published the text and English translation of the West Syrian Synodicon, which includes a version of the *Testamentum* lacking some of the liturgical materials found in other versions.[4]

FRENCH: In 1903 Francois Nau translated the entire Clementine Octateuch into French.[5] However, in so doing he combined in his translation the two

---

[1] See nos. 20 and 24 in the Bibliography.
[2] No. 25 in the Bibliography, 187-188.
[3] For more information on James of Edessa, see *Geschichte der syrische Literatur* (Marcus and Weber, Bonn: 1922; repr. de Gruyter, Berlin, 1968), 248-256.
[4] See no. 15 in the Bibliography.
[5] No. 11 in the Bibliography.

manuscript traditions of the Octateuch without distinguishing the readings of one manuscript group from another.[1] Thus, as a critical tool Nau's translation has no value.

Robert Beylot's critical edition and French translation of the Ethiopic appeared in 1984 under the title *Testamentum Domini éthiopien* (Peeters, Louvain, 1984). See above under Section VI for criticism of Beylot's edition.

IX. THIS EDITION

The present work is a translation of portions of Rahmani's Syriac text, checked against the readings of the Synodicon where applicable. The present author has tried to include as many of the *Testamentum* liturgical materials as possible, but because of limitations of space, some texts (e.g., on the love feast or offering of fruits or miscellaneous liturgical regulations) have had to be omitted. The translation aims to be as literal as possible in rendering the Syriac, while attempting to put the text in coherent modern English.

Textual notes and commentary notes accompany the translations. Because of space limitations, the number of notes included in this edition is minimal. This work is not a critical edition. The textual notes indicate where Rahmani's manuscripts contained variant readings.

Unfortunately for those who read only English, the great majority of works on the *Testamentum* are in French and German. References to these works in the commentary notes is by their number in the select bibliography which appears at the end of this introduction.

The present author hopes that these translations will stimulate new interest in this fascinating document which can shed much light on the development of liturgy, theology and church order during the century following the Peace of Constantine.

X. FURTHER QUESTIONS

The most pressing need at present is for a critical edition of the text which takes into account the different language versions. Before such a task can be accomplished, there must be critical editions of the Syriac and Arabic, in addition to a re-examinaton of Beylot's Ethiopic text. Until such critical editions appear, the questions of the *Testamentum*'s sources, provenance and authorship remain open. Another important area of research is the subsequent history of the *Testamentum* materials (liturgical and canonical) in the so-called monophysite churches.

XI. ABBREVIATIONS

AC=Apostolic Constitutions, composed ca. 375-380, vicinity of Antioch. ET: W.Jardine Grisbrooke, (ed.), *The Liturgical Portions of the Apostolic Constitutions: A Text for Students.* (Alcuin/GROW Joint Liturgical Study 13-14, Grove Books, Bramcote, Notts., 1990).

---

[1] Coquin, 168.

ApTrad=The Apostolic Tradition, date of composition unknown; commonly ascribed to St. Hippolytus of Rome, *ca.* 215. ET: Geoffrey J. Cuming, ed., *Hippolytus: A Text for Students.* (Grove Liturgical Study 8, Grove Books, Bramcote, Notts., 1976).

B=MS *Borg. syr.* 148 (ff° 61r-86r), A.D. 1576.

CH=Canons of Hippolytus, composed ca. 336-340, vicinity of Alexandria. ET: Paul F. Bradshaw (ed.), *The Canons of Hippolytus* (Alcuin/Grow Joint Liturgical Study 2, Grove Books, Bramcote, Notts., 1987).

Cn=conjectured reading.

ETH=*Testamentum Domini éthiopien*, ed. Beylot.

KRQ=Wilhelm Riedel, *Die Kirchenrechtsquellen des Patriarchats Alexandrien* (Leipzig: 1900).

LEW=F. E. Brightman, *Liturgies Eastern and Western* (Oxford, 1896, repr. 1965).

M=MS Library of the Catholic Metropolitan of Mosul (ff° 339v-348r), A.D. 1651-1652.

R=Ignatius Ephrem II Rahmani, *Testamentum Domini Nostri Jesu Christi* (Kirchheim, Mainz, 1899; repr. Georg Olms, Hildesheim, 1968).

S=Codex Sangermanensis 38, eighth century.

SYN=*The Synodicon in the West Syrian Tradition*, ed. Vööbus. Based upon MS 8/11 of the Syrian Orthodox Patriarchate of Damascus, A.D. 1204.

T=Testamentum Domini

XII. SELECT BIBLIOGRAPHY

Unfortunately for the student who reads only English, the majority of works on the *Testamentum* are in French and German. The literature on the church orders in general is out of date, and awaits a fresh examination of the major critical questions surrounding that genre.

A. TEXTS AND TRANSLATIONS

1. Baumstark, Anton. 'Eine ägyptische Mess- und Taufliturgie vermutlich des 6. Jahrhunderts' in *Oriens Christianus* 1 (1901), 1-45.
2. Beylot, Robert. *Testamentum Domini éthiopien.* (Peeters, Louvain, 1984). Review of Beylot by Roger Cowley in *Journal of Semitic Studies* 31 (1986), 292-295.
3. Burmester, O.H.E. 'The Coptic and Arabic versions of the Mystagogia' in *Muséon* 46 (1933), 203-235.
4. Cooper, James, and Arthur John Maclean. *The Testament of our Lord translated into English from the Syriac with introduction and notes.* (T. & T. Clark, London, 1902).
5. Engberding, Hieronymus. 'Untersuchungen zu den jüngst veröffentlichten Bruchstücken sa'idischer Liturgie.' in *Oriens Christianus* 43 (1959), 59-69.
6. Harden, J.M. 'The Anaphora of the Ethiopic Testament of our Lord.' in *Journal of Theological Studies* 23 (1922), 44-49.
7. Hyvernat, Henry. 'Fragmente der altkoptischen Liturgie.' in *Römische Quartelschrift* 1 (1887), 335-337.

8. de Lagarde, Paul. *Reliquiae iuris ecclesiastici antiquissimae syriace.* (Lipsiae, 1856). Pp. 2-12, 44-61.
9. —. *Reliquiae iuris ecclesiastici antiquissimae graece.* (Lipsiae, 1856). Pp. 80-89.
10. Ludolf (alias Leutholf), Job. *Historia aethiopica sive brevis et succincta descriptio regni Habessinorum.* (Francofurti ad Moenum, 1581). Pp. 341-345.
11. Nau, Francois. *La version syriaque de lOctateuque de Clément, traduit en francais.* (Paris, 1913).
12. Quasten, Johannes. *Monumenta eucharistica et liturgica vetustissima collegit, notis et prolegominis instruxit Johannes Quasten. Pars V: Ex Testamento Domini Nostri Jesu Christi.* (Hanstein, Bonn, 1935-1937).
13. Rahmani, Ignatius Ephrem II. *Testamentum Domini nostri Jesu Christi.* (Moguntiae, 1899. Repr. Georg Olms, 1968).
14. Velat, Bernard. *Études sur le me'erāf.* (Patrologia Orientalis 33. Firmin-Didot, Paris, 1966).
15. Vööbus, Arthur. *The Synodicon in the West Syrian Tradition* (Corpus Scriptorum Christianorum Orientalium 367-368, Scriptores Syri 161-162. Louvain, 1975).

STUDIES

16. Amann, E. 'Testament de Notre-Seigneur Jesus-Christ.' in *Dictionnaire de théologie catholique* XV:194-200.
17. Arendzen, J.P. 'A New Syriac Text of the Apocalyptic Part of the Testament of the Lord.' in *Journal of Theological Studies* 2 (1901), 401-411.
18. Arranz, M. 'The Functions of the Christian Assembly in the Testament of our Lord.' in *Roles in the Liturgical Assembly* (Pueblo, New York: 1981), 29-59.
19. —. 'L'ofice de la veilée nocturne dans l'Église greque et dans l'Église russe.' in *Orientalia Christiana Periodica* 42 (1976), 117-155, 402-425.
20. —. 'Le "Sancta Sanctis" dans la tradition liturgique des églises.' in *Archiv für Liturgiewissenschaft* 15 (1973), 31-67, esp. 59-60.
21. Baumstark, Anton. 'Überlieferung und Bezeugung der *diatheke tou kyriou hemon Iesou Christou.*' in *Römische Quartelschrift* 14 (1900), 1-45.
22. —. 'Die Arabischen Texte der *diatheke tou kyriou.*' in *Römische Quartelschrift* 14 (1900), 291-300.
23. Botte, Bernard. 'L'Épiclèse de l'Anaphore d'Hippolyte.' in *Recherches de théologie ancienne et médievale* 14 (1947), 241-251.
24. Bouyer, Louis. *Eucharist.* (Trans. by Charles Underhill Quinn). (University of Notre Dame Press, Notre Dame, 1968).
25. Coquin, René-Georges. 'Le *Testamentum Domini*: Problèmes de tradition textuelle.' in *Parole de l'Orient* 5 (1974), 165-188.
26. Dib, S.D. 'Les Versions Arabes du "Testamentum Domini Nostri Jesu Christi." ' in *Revue de l'Orient Chrètien* 10 (1905), 418-423.
27. Drews, Paul. 'Testamentum Domini nostri Jesu Christi.' in *Theologische Studien und Kritiken* 74 (1901), 141-170.
28. Funk, Franz Xaver. *Das Testament unseres Herrn und die verwandten Schriften.* (Forschungen zur christlichen Literatur- und Dogmengeschichte, 2. Band, 1-2. Heft. Mainz: 1901).

29. Guerrier, L., and S. Grebaut. 'Le testament en Galilee de Notre-Seigneur Jesus-Christ.' PO 9 (1913), 143-232. Review of Ethiopic text and French translation: Montague Rhodes James review in *Journal of Theological Studies* 14 (1913), 601-606.

30. Harnack, Adolf. 'Vorläufige Bemerkungen zu dem jngst syrisch und lateinisch publizierten "Testamentum Domini nostri Jesu Christi." ' in *Sitzungsberichte der Berliner Akademie der Wissenschaften* (1899), 878-891.

31. Jugie, M. 'La Messe en Orient du IVe au IXe siecle.' in *Dictionnaire de theologie catholique* X:1317-1332.

32. Kelly, Henry A. *The Devil at Baptism: Ritual, Theology and Drama.* (Cornell University Press, Ithaca and London, 1985). 139-142, 157, 192-193.

33. Kent, W.H. 'The Syriac Testament of Our Lord.' in *The Dublin Review* (1900), 245-274.

34. Leclercq, Henri. 'Messe.' in *Dictionnaire d'archéologie chrètienne et de liturgie* XI 1:622-624.

35. Ligier, Louis, S.J. 'L'anaphore de la "Tradition apostolique" dans le "Testamentum Domini." ' in: Bryan Spinks, (ed.), *The Sacrifice of Praise* (CLV-Editione Liturgiche, Rome: 1981), 89-106.

36. Morin, G. 'Le Testament du Seigneur' in *Revue Bénédictine 17* (1900), 10-28.

37. Parisot, J. 'Note sur la mystagogie du "Testament du Seigneur." ' in *Journal Asiatique*, neuvième série, 15 (1900)

38. Post, Paul. 'La Liturgie en tant qu'architecture? Remarques sur la relation entre le "Testamentum Domini Jesu Christi" et l'architecture des églises dans l'Illyricum oriental' in *Bijdragen 42* (1981), 392-420.

39. Quasten, Johannes. 'Die Ostervigil im Testamentum Domini.' in Balthasar, Fischer and Johannes Wagner, (eds.), *Paschatis Sollemnia: Studien zu Osterfeier und Osterfrömmigkeit* (Herder, Basel, 1959). Pp. 87-95.

40. Raes, Alphonse. 'Les paroles de la consecration dans les anaphores syriennes' in *Orientalia Christiana Periodica* 3, 486-504.

41. Rahmani, Ignatius Ephrem II. *Les Liturgies Orientales et Occidentales étudiées séparément et comparées entres elles.* (Beyrouth, 1929).

42. Richardson, Cyril C. 'A Note on the Epicleses in Hippolytus and the Testamentum Domini.' in *Recherches de théologie ancienne et médievale 15* (1948), 357-359.

43. —. 'The So-Called Epiclesis in Hippolytus.' in *Harvard Theological Review* 40 (1947), 101-108.

44. Schermann, Theodor, *Ägyptische Abendmahlsliturgien des ersten jahrtausends in ihrer Überlieferung dargestellt.* StGKA 6. Band, Heft 1-2. (Paderborn, 1912).

45. Schmidt, C. *Gespräche Jesu mit seinen Jüngern nach der Auferstehung. Ein katholisch-apostolisches Sendschreibendes 2. Jahrhunderts.* Texte und Untersuchungen 43. (Leipzig, 1919). 157-166.

46 Taft, Robert, S.J. *The Great Entrance.* 2ed. Orientalia Christiana Analecta 200. (Pont. Institutum Studiorum Orientalium, Rome, 1978).

47. von der Goltz, Eduard Freiherrn, ed. *De Virginitate: Eine echte Schrift des Athanasius.* Texte und Untersuchungen 29, Heft 2a. (Hinrichs, Leipzig, 1905).

48. Wordsworth, J. 'The Testament of Our Lord' in *Internationale theologische Zeitschrift* 8 (1900), 452-472.

49. Zahn, Theodore. 'Neue Funde aus der alten Kirche 4. "Das neue Testament unseres Herrn." ' in *Neue kirchliche Zeitschrift* 11 (1900), 438-450.

1. Eucharist (I.23, 24, 35; II.10)

As in **ApTrad**, the *Testamentum* contains two descriptions of the eucharistic rite, one following the account of episcopal ordination (I.23), the other following the baptismal liturgy (II.10; see section on Initiation for texts).

Of all the *Testamentum* liturgical materials, the eucharistic prayer has received the most attention from historians of liturgy. A number of features make the *Testamentum* anaphora noteworthy. The prayer lacks the Sanctus, it does not contain the dominical word over the cup, and its intercessions are primitive. The exact form of the prayers epiklesis is open to question, and was the subject of a debate between Bernard Botte and Cyril Richardson in the 1940s (see the Notes to this section for citation of the literature). This question continues to bear upon that of the form of the epiklesis in the version of **ApTrad** the *Testamentum* has used as its source.

How the compiler has used the **ApTrad** anaphora is open to debate. Many authors view the T anaphora as a mere amplification of that in **ApTrad**. Ligier sees the T prayer as the result of a recasting of the **ApTrad** anaphora in the mould of the *collaudatio* form of prayer found elsewhere in the *Testamentum*.

Scholars have paid less attention to the rest of the T eucharistic rite, which contains a number of interesting features, including a version of the diaconal *ektene* (I.35), the diaconal admonition before the anaphora (I.23), private prayers after receiving (I.23), and the presence of women at the altar at the time of the celebration (I.23).

[I.23: The Eucharistic Liturgy]
On the Sabbath let him [i.e., the bishop] offer three breads for the fullness[1] of the Trinity. On Sunday let him offer four breads for the fullness of the Gospel.

Because the ancient people went astray, when he offers let the veil in front of the door be drawn. Within it let him offer together with the presbyters, deacons and canonical widows and subdeacons and deaconesses, readers who possess

----

I.23 = **ApTrad** 4. T has removed the **ApTrad** connection of the eucharistic rite with the ordination of the bishop. **Sabbath and Sunday**] Taft, 'The Frequency of the Eucharist throughout History,' notes that by the time of Patriarch Timothy II of Alexandria (381-385) and John Cassian (cs. 400), the eucharist was being celebrated on Saturday and Sunday. In Robert Taft, *Beyond East and West* (Pastoral Press, Washington: 1984), 63. Canon 49 of the Council of Laodicea makes Saturday and Sunday the only times the eucharist may be offered during Lent. **veil**] Lev 16.2, 21.23.

[1] 'Fullness': the Syriac can also mean 'completion, fulfilling, satisfying.'

[spiritual] gifts.[1] Let the bishop stand first in the midst [of them] and the presbyters immediately after him; after them, the widows immediately behind the presbyters on the left side, the deacons behind the presbyters on the right side, then the readers behind them, the subdeacons behind the readers, the deaconesses behind the subdeacons.

Let the bishop place his hand upon the breads which have been placed upon the altar in this way, the presbyters placing [their hands on the breads] at the same time. Let the rest be standing only.

Let the bread of the catechumens[2] not be received, not even if he has a believing son or wife and wants to offer on their behalf. Let him not offer until he is baptized.

Before the bishop or presbyter offers, let the people give the Peace to each other. Then, when there is a great silence, let the deacon say as follows:

[Admonition of the Deacon over the Eucharist[3]]

[Let] your hearts [be] in heaven.
If anyone bears a grudge[4] against his neighbour, let him be reconciled.
If anyone has a faithless mind[5], let him confess.
If anyone has a mind foreign to the commandments, let him depart.
If anyone has fallen into sin[6], let him not hide. He cannot hide.
If anyone has infirm reasoning, let him not draw near.
If anyone is defiled, if anyone is not steadfast[7], let him give place.
If anyone is a stranger to the commandments of Jesus, let him depart.
If anyone treats the prophets with contempt, let him separate himself. Let him deliver himself from the wrath of the Only-begotten.
Let us not despise the Cross.[8]
Let us avoid threatening.
We have our Lord [as] spectator, the Father of lights with the Son; the angels are visiting.[9]
Look to yourselves, that you are not bearing a grudge against those near you.
See that no one is angry: God sees.

---

widows behind the presbyters] this prescription directly contradicts Canon 44 of the Council of Laodicea, which forbade women going to the altar. **Admonition]** Unique to T. **Father of lights]** Jas 1.17. **The angels are visiting]** Similar to a line in the diaconal admonition of I.35.

[1] Readers ... gifts: Rahmani **cn**: readers, [and] those who possess [spiritual] gifts.
[2] catechumens: Rahmani **cn**: a catechumen.
[3] Gk *eucharistia* transliterated.
[4] bears a grudge: or: is angry.
[5] mind: or: conscience.
[6] fallen ... sin: lit., is in a falling of sin.
[7] Or: sure.
[8] Or: treat the Cross with contempt.
[9] threatening ... angels visiting: **B** reads: Let us avoid the threatening of our Lord. We have a spectator, the Father of lights ... etc.

Lift up your hearts to offer for the salvation of life and holiness.
In the wisdom of God let us receive the grace which has been bestowed
upon us.

[I.23. Anaphora.]
Then let the bishop, confessing and giving thanks, say with[1] a loud voice:
Our Lord be with you.
And let the people say: And with your spirit.
Let the bishop say: Lift up your hearts.
Let the people say: They are with the Lord.
Let the bishop say: Let us give thanks to the Lord.
And let all the people say: It is meet and right.
And let the bishop cry out: Holy things for holy people.
And let the people shout: In heaven and on earth without end.

EUCHARIST[2], OR THANKSGIVING OVER THE OFFERING[3]

[The eucharistic prayer. Preface]
We give you thanks, O God, the Holy One and confirmer of our souls, giver of
our life, treasure of incorruptibility, and Father of your Only-begotten, our
Saviour, whom you sent to us in the last times as Saviour and proclaimer of your
will. For it is your will that we be saved in you. Our heart gives you thanks, O
Lord, [our] mind, [our] soul, along with every thought, that your grace, O Lord,
may come upon us, [so] that we may praise you continually, and your Only-
begotten, and your Holy Spirit, now and always and to the ages of ages.
Amen.[4]

You, Lord, [are] the power of the Father, the grace of the nations, knowledge,
true wisdom, exaltation of the meek, medicine of souls.[5] [You are] the confidence of us who believe, for you are the strengthening of the righteous, the
hope of the persecuted, the harbour of those who are buffeted, the illuminator of
the perfect.[6]

Anaphora=ApTrad 4. Unlike CH, T retains the ApTrad anaphora. T's redaction
involves not extensive rewriting, but rather expansion of the ApTrad prayer using discrete blocs of material which more than doubles the size of the prayer. Holy things
for holy people] Unlike other eucharistic rites, which place the Sancta Sanctis before
communion, T places it before the anaphora. For a discussion of the Sancta Sanctis in
the *Testamentum*, see: Arranz, Bibliography No.20, particularly 59-60. Arranz
understands the Sancta Sanctis here as relating to the confession of sin before the
offering, and to the particular T concern with the purity of those offering the
eucharist.

[1] Or: in.
[2] Gk *eucharistia* transliterated.
[3] M reads: offerings.
[4] O Lord, [our] mind . . . ages of ages. Amen.: only in Syriac.
[5] Or: medicine of the meek, exaltation of souls.
[6] Or: mature.

O Son of the living God, make to shine upon us from your gift which cannot be inquired into, fortitude, valour, confidence, wisdom, steadfastness, unlapsing faith, unshaken hope, knowledge of your Spirit, meekness, integrity, so that always we your servants, Lord, and all the people may purely praise you, bless you, give you thanks at all times, Lord, and supplicate you.

And also let the bishop say:

You, Lord, [are] the founder of the heights and King of the luminous treasuries, visitor of the heavenly Zion, King of the archangelic orders: of dominions, praises, thrones, raiments, lights, joys, delights. [You are] Father of kings, you who hold all things in your hand, you who provide by your thought[1], through your Only-begotten Son who was crucified for our sins. You, Lord, being pleased with him, sent your Word, who is the son of your counsel and son of your promise, through whom you made all things, into a virgin womb; who when he was conceived and became incarnate, being born from the Holy Spirit and the Virgin, was shown to be your Son, who, fulfilling your will and preparing a holy people, stretched out his hands to suffering so that he might free those who have hoped in you from sufferings and corruption of death,

[The eucharistic prayer. Institution narrative.]

who, when when he was betrayed to voluntary suffering so that he might set straight those who had stumbled, and find the lost, and raise the dead, and undo[2] death, and burst the bonds of the devil, and fulfil the will of the Father, and tread upon Sheol, and open a way of life, and lead the righteous to light, and fix a boundary, and lighten the darkness, and nurture infants, and reveal the Resurrection, taking bread, he gave [it] to his disciples, saying, 'Take, eat; this is my body which is broken for you for the forgiveness of sins. When you do this, you make my resurrection'. Also the cup of wine which he mixed he gave for a type of the blood which he shed for us.

Praise you, bless you ... supplicate you] Phrases with the same series of verbs appear in the daily prayers of I.26. On the basis of this commonality between the daily prayers and the anaphora, L. Ligier, Bib. No. 35, suggested that the **T** anaphora was the product of the recasting of the **ApTrad** anaphora into the mould of the Syrian *collaudatio*. **You make my resurrection**] Many commentators have suggested that here the Syriac translator has confused Gk *anamnesis* for *anastasis*. However, if James of Edessa did indeed translate the Gk text into Syriac, it is difficult to believe that such an accomplished translator as James could have made such a mistake. The reading 'resurrection' here makes some sense within the context of the **T** emphasis upon the resurrection (e.g., prayer at midnight because it was the hour of the resurrection (I.31). The Mystagogy of I.28 which narrates the work of Christ in Hades.) **The cup of wine**] The **T** institution narrative is remarkable for its lack of the dominical word over the cup. Both the Ethiopic **T** and the Ethiopic Anaphora of Our Lord preserve this feature of the prayer. According to Raes in Bib. No. 40, the only Syriac anaphoras whose insitution narratives lack the dominical cup-word are John of Haran and Matthew the Pastor.

[1] Or: rule by your reason.
[2] Or: loose.

And also let him say:

Remembering, therefore, your death and resurrection, we offer you bread and cup, thanking you who alone are the eternal God and our Saviour, since you have promised to us to stand before you and serve you as priests. For this we give you thanks, we your servants, O Lord.
And let the people say likewise.

[The eucharistic prayer. Oblation.]

And also let him say:

We offer you this thanksgiving, eternal Trinity, Lord Jesus Christ, Lord Father, from whom all creation and every nature trembles, fleeing into itself; Lord Holy Spirit, we have brought this drink and this food of your holiness; make it be for us not for condemnation, not for reproach, not for destruction, but for the healing [and] support of our spirit. Indeed, O God, grant us that through your Name every thought of what is unpleasing to you may flee. Lord, grant that every proud thought may be driven away by your Name written within the veil of your lofty sanctuaries, [your Name, at] which Sheol, hearing [it], is dismayed. [By your Name] the depth is rent, spirits are expelled, the dragon is crushed, unbelief is driven away, disobedience is subdued, anger is appeased, jealousy achieves nothing, arrogance is reproved, avarice is uprooted, boastfulness is removed, pride is brought low, and every nature giving birth to bitterness is destroyed.

[The eucharistic prayer. Intercessions and Doxology.]

Therefore, O Lord, allow our inner eyes to see you, praising and glorifying you, commemorating you, serving you, having a portion in you alone. O Son and Word of God, to whom all things are subdued, sustain to the end those who have [spiritual] gifts of revelations. Make firm those who have a gift of healing; embolden those who have the power of tongues; direct those who have the word of teaching; care always for those who do your will; visit the widows, succour the orphans, remember those who have fallen asleep in the faith, and grant us an inheritance with your saints, and bestow upon us the power to please you, just as they were pleasing to you. Shepherd the people in uprightness. Sanctify us all, O God; grant that all those who partake [and] receive your holy things may be united with you, that they may be filled with the Holy Spirit for the confirmation of faith in truth, so that they may always offer you a doxology, and your beloved Son Jesus Christ, through whom to you be praise and power with your Holy Spirit, to the ages of ages.
And let the people say amen.

We offer you this thanksgiving] The text of the T anaphoral oblation is preserved in Sahidic, Syriac and Ethiopic. The critical problems surrounding this portion of the text are numerous, and have yet to be completely answered. The most thorough analysis of the problems surrounding the interrelationship of all the above versions is that of H. Engberding, Bib. No. 5. **Lord Holy Spirit]** For the literature surrounding the debate over the epiklesis in the T anaphora and its relation to the **ApTrad** anaphora, see Bib. Nos. 23, 42 and 43.

[I.23. Post-anaphora.]

Deacon: Let us earnestly beseech our Lord and our God, that he bestow upon us *homonoia*[1] of spirit.

Bishop: Give us *homonoia* in the Holy Spirit, and heal our souls through this offering, that we may live in you in all the ages of ages.

People: Amen.

Let the people also pray in the same [words].

And after these things, let the seal of the thanksgiving [be] thus:

Blessed be the name of the Lord for ever. People: amen.

Priest: Blessed is he who has come[2] in the name of the Lord. Blessed [be] the name of his glory.

And let all the people say: So be it, so be it, so be it.

Let the bishop say: Send the grace of the Spirit upon us.

If the bishop has a wet dream[3] let him not offer[4], but let the presbyter offer. Nor let him partake of the mystery, not as if he were pollutes,[5] but because of the honour of the altar. But after he fasts[6] and washes in pure water, let him come near and minister.[7] Similarly also [for] a presbyter. Also, if a widow is menstruous, let her not come near. Similarly if a woman or lay person or anyone else from the *qyāmā*[8] [is polluted][9], let him not approach because of the honour [of the altar], unless after fasting[10] and washing.

Post-anaphora: This material is unique to **T**. **If the bishop]** This canonical material focusing upon the purity of those presiding at the eucharist seems to be derived from Lev 15. Arranz, Bib. No. 20, hypothesizes that this type of legislation, found elsewhere in the document, may derive from a Judeo-Christian source used by **T**. **Qyāmā]** College or class. Exactly to whom the document refers here is unclear. Before the ordination of a presbyter (I.30) the document speaks of the 'priestly *qyāmā*,' which may include all those from the community allowed within the veil of the altar. See above, in the introductory rubrics to I.23, and immediately below. **Let the priests receive]** By 'priests' (Syriac *kāhnē*) **T** obviously means the entire membership of the clerical class within the community. Perhaps here we have an enumeration of the members of the 'priestly *qyāmā*' mentioned above. **T** contains words for both 'priest' and 'presbyter'. This translation always translates the Syriac *kāhnā* by 'priest' and the Syriac *qashishā* as 'presbyter'.

1 Translation of Gk *homonoia*; thus wherever *homonoia* appears in the text.

2 B: comes

3 Lit., a dream of coition.

4 Or: draw near.

5 Or: defiled.

6 Or: abstains.

7 Or: serve.

8 SYN: *bnai gyāmā* ('sons of the covenant').

9 SYN: shall see a dream of coition.

10 Or: abstaining.

Let the priests[1] receive first in the following way: bishop, presbyters, deacons, widows,[2] readers, subdeacons. After them, those who have [spiritual] gifts, the newly baptized, little children. The people [receive] in the following way: the elderly, virgins. After them, the rest. The women [receive in the following way]: deaconesses, after them, the rest.[3]

Let each one, when he receives the thanksgiving, say amen before partaking.

Afterwards, let him [or her] pray in the following way; after he receives from the eucharist[4] let him say:

Holy, Holy, Holy, ineffable Trinity. Grant me to receive this body for life, not for condemnation. And grant me to bear fruits[5] pleasing to you, that I may appear pleasing to you. May I live in you as I perform your commandments, and may I call you Father with courage. When I call [down] upon myself your kingdom and your will, may your name be sanctified in me, because you are mighty and glorious, and praise [be] to you forever. Amen.

After the prayer, let him [or her] receive.

When he receives the cup, let him say amen two times for the fullness of the body and blood.

After all have received let them pray, confessing and giving thanks for receiving,[6] while the deacon says:

Praise the Lord when we receive his holy things, that the reception may be for our own life and salvation. We pray and beseech, raising a doxology[7] to the Lord our God.

Then the bishop:

Lord, giver of eternal light, pilot of our souls, guide of the holy: give us understanding[8] eyes which always heed you, and ears which listen to you alone, that our soul may be filled with your grace. Form in us a pure heart, [O] God, that we may always recognize your greatness.[9] Wondrous God, and lover of humankind[10]: amend our souls; through this eucharist[11] we receive establish our minds [to be] undeviating, we your unworthy[12] servants. For blessed is your Kingdom, Lord God, and praised and glorified in the Father and in the Son and in the

Holy, holy, holy] This prayer appears in the Coptic Jacobite and Ethiopic Jacobite eucharistic liturgies (LEW 185.27-38 and 241.8-21). **Lord, giver of eternal**] The Ethiopic Jacobite liturgy refers to this prayer (LEW 243.9).

[1] priests: SYN omits.
[2] SYN: widows who have been consecrated.
[3] women . . . the rest: SYN omits.
[4] Gk *eucharistia* transliterated; afterwards . . . eucharist: SYN omits.
[5] Lit., produce fruits.
[6] Lit., for the reception.
[7] The Syriac here has a calque for Gk *doxologia*.
[8] Or: intellectual.
[9] M: greatness of God. Wondrous, and lover of humankind . . .
[10] Transliteration of Gk *philanthropos*.
[11] Gk *eucharistia* transliterated.
[12] unworthy: or: poor, humble.

Holy Spirit, both from before the ages, and now and always, and for ever and ever, and to the unending ages of ages.

People: amen.

[I.24. Blessing of Oil.]

If there is oil for the healing of those who suffer, let it be sanctified in the following way. Let him say quietly, setting the vessel before the altar:

Lord God, you who bestowed on us the Spirit, the Paraclete: Lord, [whose] name is salvific and unshaken, hidden to the foolish but revealed to the wise: Christ, you who have sanctified and made wise in your mercy us your servants whom you in your wisdom have chosen, who sent the knowledge of your Spirit to us sinners through[1] your holiness, when you bestowed the power of the Spirit upon us, you are the healer of all who are ill and all who suffer. You who gave the gift of healing to those you deemed worthy of this [gift]: send the deliverance[2] of your compassion upon this oil which is a type[3] of your richness[4], that it may deliver those who are diseased, and [that] it may heal the sick and sanctify those who return, as they draw near to your faith.[5]

For you are powerful and glorious[6] for ever and ever.

People: amen.

[I.25. Blessing of Water.]

Similarly, the same [prayer] over water.

[I.35. The Diaconal Ektene]

In all things, let him [i.e., the deacon] be the eye of the church, informing [the bishop] with fear. In like manner let him be a type of *eusebia*.[7]

Let him announce[8] in this way:

[Admonition of the Deacon[9]]

Let us rise.

Let everyone know his place.

I.24 = ApTrad 5. Although I.24 covers the same subject as ApTrad 5, the T prayer is completely different from that in ApTrad. ApTrad 5 also does not mention the blessing of water. Sarapion 5 has a 'Prayer over the offerings of oils and waters.' See also AC VIII.28. **when you bestowed**] cf. Jn. 20.22-23, Acts 2.1-4. **those who return**] a reference, perhaps, to the use of sanctified oil at the reconciliation of penitents, which does not otherwise appear in T. I.35 = Unique to T.

1 Or: by
2 Or: salvation
3 Syriac: *tupsā*
4 Lit., type of your fatness
5 A reference to the use of the sanctified oil at the reconciliation of penitents.
6 Or: praised
7 The Syriac here has a calque for Gk *eusebia*
8 Or: admonish
9 M reads: deacons

Let the catechumens depart.
See that no one defiled, no one excommunicate [remains].
Lift up the eyes of your hearts.
The angels are watching.
See [that] he who does not trust departs.
Let us make supplication with concord of mind[1]
[Let] no fornicator, no one who is angry [remain]; if someone is a servant of evil, let him withdraw.
See [that] we beseech [God] as sons of light.
Let us supplicate our Lord and God and saviour Jesus Christ.

As the presbyter or bishop[2] begins the prayer, let the people pray and kneel.[3] Then let the deacon say as follows:

For the peace from above let us beseech, that the Lord, in his mercy, may grant us peace.

For our faith let us beseech, that the Lord may grant that we steadfastly keep faith in him until the end.

For unity and *homonoia* let us beseech, that the Lord may keep us all together in the *homonoia* of the Spirit.

For patience let us beseech, that the Lord may impart patience in all sufferings, until the end.

For the apostles let us supplicate, that the Lord may grant us to please him as they pleased him, and that we be deemed worthy of their inheritance.

For the holy prophets let us beseech, that the Lord may number us among them.

For the holy confessors let us beseech, that the Lord God may grant us to end [our lives] in the same mind [as theirs].

For the bishop let us beseech, that our Lord may give him long life in faith for us, [that he] rightly determine the word of truth and purely and blamelessly stand at the head of the church.

For the presbyterate let us beseech, that the Lord not take away from them the spirit of the presbyterate; may he bestow diligence and piety upon them until the end.

For the deacons let us beseech, that the Lord grant them to run a perfect race, and to bring holiness to perfection[4] and [that the Lord] remember their labour and charity.

---

no one defiled] Another example of the **T** emphasis upon purity at the altar. See above, I.23. **The angels are watching]** A similar phrase concerning the angelic spectators of the liturgy occurs in the deacon's admonition over the eucharist in I.23. **Concord of mind]** References to the *homonoia* of the congregation occur elsewhere in **T** (cf. I.23).

[1] Translation of Gk *homonoia*.
[2] Gk *episkopos* transliterated
[3] Or: genuflect
[4] Or: to accomplish holiness, learn holiness by heart

For the female presbyters let us beseech, that the Lord hear their supplications and in the grace of the Spirit perfectly keep their hearts [and] support their labour.

For the subdeacons, readers and deaconesses let us beseech, that the Lord grant them to receive [their] wage in patience.

For the worldly[1] faithful let us beseech, that the Lord grant them to keep faith perfectly.

For the catechumens let us beseech, that the Lord grant them to be made worthy for the bath of forgiveness, and sanctify them with the seal of holiness.

For the kingdom let us beseech, that the Lord bestow peace upon it.

For the exalted authorities let us beseech, that the Lord grant them understanding and fear of him.

For the entire world let us beseech, that the Lord attend to each one as is suitable.

For those who sail and travel on roads, let us beseech, that the Lord may direct them[2] with the right hand of mercies.

For the persecuted let us beseech, that the Lord may grant them patience and knowledge [and] also bestow upon them mature[3] labour.

For those who have fallen asleep from the church let us beseech, that the Lord bestow upon them a place of rest.

For those who have fallen let us beseech, that the Lord not remember their transgressions, but mitigate the threat from them.[4]

And we all who are in need of prayer beseech, that the Lord keep us and protect us with a spirit of peace.

Let us petition and beseech the Lord, that he receive our prayers.

After the deacon commemorates, let the bishop make a sign with his hand.

Let the deacon say:
Let us rise in the Holy Spirit, that, as we are instructed, we may increase in his grace, boasting in his name, built upon the foundation of the apostles. Let us pray [and] beseech the Lord, that, being persuaded, he may receive our prayers.

Then let the bishop finish[5] [the prayer]. And let the people say amen.

Labour] A favourite T word, which often refers to the work of prayer by the bishop and widows. **Female presbyters]** Some authors identify these members of the clergy who rank immediately after the deacons as the so-called 'widows who sit in front' who play such an important role in T. Canon 11 of the Council of Laodicea treats the matter of female presbyters, who were active in fourth century Asia Minor. This petition adds weight to arguments proposing Asia Minor as the provenance of T. **Seal of holiness]** The text suggests not only the water bath but a (post-baptismal?) anointing. **Built]** Eph. 2.20.

[1] Or: secular
[2] them: **B** omits
[3] Or: perfect
[4] Or: to them
[5] Or: complete

2. Christian Initiation (II.5-10)

The *Testamentum* contains a complete liturgy of initiation in Book Two of the Syriac (II. 7-10). The framework of the rite derives from some version of the ApTrad, but the *Testamentum* has greatly augmented the ApTrad rite with long prayers of exorcism over the candidates (II. 7), prayer that the candidates might be worthy to receive the Holy Spirit (II.9), the renunciation and the *syntaxis* (adhesion) before baptism. For a discussion of the *Testamentum* exorcisms, see H.A. Kelley, Bib. No. 32.

- -

[II.5.]

After the catechumens have prayed, let the bishop or presbyter, laying a hand upon them, say the prayer of handlaying of the catechumens.

[Prayer of the Catechumens]

God, who sends thunderings and causes lightnings[1], you who established the heaven and spread forth the earth, and who enlightens the faithful, and restores[2] those who stray; you who restored the dead to life and gave hope to those who had none; and freed the entire world[3] from error through[4] the descent of your Only-begotten Son Jesus Christ: hear us, Lord[5], and give these souls understanding[6], perfection, undoubting faith, knowledge of the truth, that they may be in a greater rank[7] than this. Through your holy name and [the name] of your beloved Son Jesus our Lord. Through him be praise and honour to you and[8] the Holy Spirit now and always and to all ages forever. Amen.
After these things, let them be dismissed.

If someone is apprehended because of my name while a catechumen, and is condemned to tortures and hastens and presses to receive the bath, let the

---

II.5 = ApTrad 19. T has expanded the **ApTrad** chapter with the inclusion of a prayer over the catechumens only alluded to in the source. **bishop or presbyter]** In **ApTrad**, the teacher of the catechumens lays a hand on them. **hastens and presses]** This phrase does not appear in **ApTrad**. The passage could be interpreted to imply that in the time of **T**, while arrest of catechumens was still a possibility, there sometimes was a space of time between their arrest and execution.

[1] Or: prepares lightnings
[2] Or: convert; lit., and you restore (or: convert)
[3] Translation of Gk *oikoumene*
[4] Or: by
[5] Lord: **B** omits
[6] Or: intelligence, intellect
[7] Or: degree
[8] and: SYN: with

shepherd[1] not hesitate, but let him give it.[2] But if he is violently killed before he is baptized,[3] let him not consider. For being baptized in his own blood justifies [him].

[II.6.]

Let every one chosen to receive the bath first be tried[4] and investigated, [as to] how they conducted themselves while catechumens: if they honoured the widows, if they visited the sick, if they walked in all humility and love, if they were diligent in good works. But let them be approved by the testimony from those who bring them.[5]

Each day, after they have heard the Gospel, let a hand be placed on them. Let them be exorcized from the day they are chosen. Let them be baptized in the days of Pascha. As the days approach,[6] let the bishop exorcize each of them individually by himself, so that he is persuaded he[7] is pure. But if it happens that he is not pure, or he has an impure[8] spirit, let him [i.e. the catechumen] be convicted by that impure[9] spirit.

Now if someone is found [to be] under such suspicion, let him be taken away from the midst [of those being exorcized] and let him be reproved and reproached, because he has not faithfully[10] heard the word of the commandments and of the admonition, because of his remaining in an evil and alien spirit.

Let those about to receive the bath be instructed on the Thursday of the last week only, washing and sprinkling their heads. If any woman at that time[11] is menstruous,[12] let her add another day [to her preparation], fasting[13] and bathing beforehand. Let them fast on both the Friday and Saturday.

Let him not consider] Rahmani translates: *ne perplexus sit.* I.e., let the bishop not worry about the salvation of the catechumen.

II.6 = ApTrad 20. the days of Pascha] Not in **ApTrad, CH**. How many days are meant here is unclear. II.8 mentions the 40 days of Pascha, which probably refers to the same period. **instructed on the Thursday of the last week only]** ApTrad and CH do not mention instruction on the Thursday before Easter. The reference to the last week only suggests that the final instruction before baptism was not to begin before that day. Canon 46 of the Council of Laodicea discusses the recitation of the Creed by the candidates on the 'fifth day of the week'; which week is meant is not clear. **menstruous]** ApTrad and CH both require the menstruous woman to put off her baptism for another time. **Let them fast]** ApTrad and CH both prescribe only a Friday fast, in contrast to Canon 50 of the Council of Laodicea, which prescribes fasting for the entire Lenten season.

[1] Or: bishop
[2] i.e., baptism
[3] Lit., while not receiving the bath
[4] Or: proved
[5] I.e., sponsor them for baptism
[6] Or: draw near
[7] I.e., the one to be baptized
[8] Or: polluted
[9] Impure: **B** omits
[10] Or: in faith
[11] at that time: **M** omits
[12] Lit., is in [her] customary flux
[13] Or: abstaining

[II.7. Exorcism over Catechumens.]

Then on the Sabbath let the bishop gather those who are going to receive the bath, and let him command [them] to kneel, while the deacon proclaims. And when there is silence, he places a hand upon them; let him exorcize [them], saying:

[Exorcism before the Bath]

O God of heaven, God of lights, God of the archangels who are under your power; God of the angels who are under your might, King[1] of Glories and of dominions; God of saints, Father of our Lord Jesus Christ, you who have freed those souls who were fettered by death; you who enlightened the one who was bound and fixed in darkness through the fixing [on the Cross] of the Passion of your Only-begotten; you who have dissolved our bonds, and removed the weight from us; you who have thrust out from us all the battle of the Evil One:

O Son and Word of God, you who have made us immortal by [2]your death, you who have glorified us with your glory; you who have loosed all the bindings of our sins by your Passion; you who have borne the curse of our sins by your Cross, and taught [that] passing over from humanity, they might become gods through your Resurrection; you who bore our wound upon yourself[3]; you who made a path to heaven for us, you who changed us from corruption to incorruptibility:

Hear me, O Lord, who in pain and fear calls out to you, Lord God and Father of our Lord Jesus Christ, before him before whom stand holy powers of the archangels, and cherubim[4] and countless hosts of princes and of seraphim. The veil of your gate is light, and fire is before your face. The throne of your glory is ineffable; the habitations of your delights which you have prepared for your saints are inexpressible; whose raiments and treasures are visible to you alone and to your holy angels; before whom all things tremble and praise [you]; your gaze measures the mountains, and your name , when spoken, rends the abysses asunder; the heavens conceal you, while they are encompassed by your hand. [I call out to you] from whom the sea and the dragons in it tremble; from whom wild animals tremble, by whose hands the mountains and the expanses of the

---

II.7 = ApTrad 20. The obvious T addition to the ApTrad text is the lengthy exorcism which fleshes out the ApTrad prescription of an exorcism on the Saturday before baptism. **proclaims**] the deacon's proclamation is not mentioned in ApTrad. **God of lights**] Jas. 1.17. **King of glories . . . dominions**] Col. 1.16. **corruption to incorruptibility**] The T emphasis upon the incorruptibility of Christ, and of those saved by him, has led some authors to suggest that T emanated from an aphthartodocetist community, perhaps one associated with Apollinaris of Laodicea. **Before whom all things tremble . . . earth**] Note the similarity between this paragraph and the *oblatio* of the anaphora.

[1] SYN: God of glories
[2] Or: at
[3] SYN adds: and healed us
[4] Gk *cheroubim* transliterated

earth waste away in fear; on account of your power the winter storm quakes and trembles, and the angry whirlwind guards its boundaries; on account of it the fire of vengeance does not transgress that which has been commanded it, but abides when constrained by your commandment; he who on whose account all creation groans with groans, commanded to wait until her time; from whom all nature and [every] creature flees in opposition; on account of whom the entire host of the enemy is subdued, and the slanderer lies fallen, and the serpent is trampled, and the dragon is killed; on account of whom the nations who have confessed you are enlightened and are strengthened by you, Lord; on your account life is revealed, and hope confirmed, and faith strengthened and the Gospel proclaimed; on account of whom corruption is brought to nought, and incorruptibility is strengthened; by whose hands humanity was formed from the earth, but once having believed in you, he is no longer earth;

Lord God almighty, I adjure these [people] by your Name, and [the name] of your beloved Son Jesus Christ. Drive out from the souls of these your servants all disease and illness, and every stumbling-block and all unbelief, all doubt and all contempt, every unclean spirit working [in them]: dumb, a murderer under the earth; fiery, dark, putrid smelling; incantational, desirous, gold-loving, proud, money-loving, wrathful.

Yes, Lord God[1], cause the arms of the devil to cease from these your servants whose names have been named by you[2]; [cause to cease] fire-worship, sorcery, idolatry, divination, astrology, necromancy, star-watching [observation], astronomy, pleasure of passions, love of obscene things, sadness, love of money, drunkenness, fornication, adultery, wantonness, presumption, quarrelsomeness, anger, confusion, evil, evil opinion.

Yes, Lord God, answer me and breathe upon these your servants the Spirit of peace , that, guarded by you, they may bring forth in you fruits of faith, virtue, wisdom, purity, self-discipline[3], perseverance, hope, *homonoia*, chastity, praise, because you have called them servants in the Name of Jesus Christ, being baptized in the Trinity, in the Name of the Father and of the Son and of the Holy Spirit, the angels, glories, dominions, the entire heavenly host being witnesses. O Lord, the *qnōmā* of their and our lives, guard their hearts, O God, because you are powerful and glorious, to all the ages of ages.

And let all the people, also the priests, say: Amen. So be it, so be it, so be it.

And if any one be in endurance[4] of anything, [or if anyone should] stand suddenly while the bishop speads, and weeps or cries out or foams at the mouth or

---

all creation groans] Rom. 8.22. **Spirit of peace**] Cf. Mt. 11.26, I Clement 60.3. **self-discipline**] Vööbus translates as 'asceticism.' One example of the ascetic terminology which **T** contains; see also I.44. *qnōmā*] The Syriac word for Gk *hypostasis*. **signing**] ApTrad mentions only a signation of forehead, ears and nose, while **CH** mentions the same body parts as **T**, but in a different order (breast, forehead, ears, nose).

[1] MS **B**, SYN: my God
[2] Or: in you
[3] Or: asceticism
[4] Or: continuance

gnashes his teeth, or gazes harshly, or is greatly lifted-up, or completely flees, being quickly carried off, let him who is [behaving] like this be hidden by the deacons so that there is no commotion while the bishop speaks. And let him who is like this be exorcized by the priests until he is purified [or: cleansed]. And so let him be baptized.

After the priest exorcizes those who have come near [or: have been brought near], or him who is found impure [or: unclean], let the priest breathe on them, signing[1] them between their eyes, on the nose, on the heart, on the ears, and so let him [i.e., the priest] raise them up.

[II. 8. The Baptismal Liturgy]

In the forty days of Pascha[2] let the people abide in the temple, keeping vigil and praying, listening to the scriptures and hymns, and [to] the sermons of teaching.[3] But on the last Saturday let them rise early, and[4] when the catechumens are exorcized until the middle of the night [on] Saturday. Let those to be baptized bring nothing except one bread for the eucharist.[5]

Let them be baptized thus: When they come to the water, let the water be pure and flowing. First the infants, then the men, then the women. However, if someone wishes to approach as to virginity, let that person first be baptized by the bishop's hand.

Let the women loose their hair when they are baptized. Let all those children who can give answer in the baptism make the response after the priest. But if they cannot, let their parents or someone from their families reply on their behalf.

But when those being baptized descend, after they respond and speak, let the bishop see if there be any man having a gold ring or a woman wearing[6] gold upon herself among them. For it is not fitting for one to have anything foreign in the water with him, but let him hand it over to those surrounding him.

But when they are ready to receive the oil for anointing, let the bishop pray over it and give thanks. But let him exorcize the other (which is for catechumens) with an exorcism. And let the deacon carry that which is exorcized, and let the presbyter stand near him. Let him, then, who stands near that of the oil over which have been given thanks be on the right, but he who stands near that [oil] which has been exorcized, on the left.

II.8 = ApTrad 21. Forty days of Pascha] In T, the forty days before Easter have not yet become fast days, but days of vigil and praying. **middle of the night on Saturday]** cf. AC V.19.3. **as to virginity]** There is evidence that in the early Syrian baptismal tradition, baptism was the rite of initiation into the 'sons of the covenant' (Syriac *bnai qyāmā*), who lived lives of virginity and asceticism. See: R. Murray, *New Testament Studies* 21 (1974), 59-80.

[1] Or: sealing
[2] Gk *pascha* transliterated
[3] Or: catechetical instructions
[4] **B:** omits
[5] Gk *eucharistia* transliterated
[6] Lit., having

And when he takes hold of each one let him ask (the one being baptized turning toward the west), and let him say, 'Say, "I renounce you, Satan, and all your service, and your theatres, and your pleasures, and all your works."' And when he has said these things and confessed, let him be anointed with that oil which was exorcized, while he who anoints him says thus: 'I anoint [with] this oil of exorcism for deliverance from every evil and unclean spirit, and for deliverance from every evil.' And also let him say ([the bishop] turning him [the baptizand] toward the east), 'I submit to you, Father and Son and Holy Spirit, from whom all nature quakes and trembles. Grant that I may do all your wishes, without fault.' Then after these things let him hand him over to the presbyter who baptizes. And let them stand stripped, in the midst of the water. Then let a deacon[1] descend with him in like manner. As he who is to be baptized is descending into the water, let him who baptizes him say thus as he lays his hand upon him:

'Do you believe in God the Father omnipotent?'
And let the one being baptized say, 'I believe.' Let him baptize him immediately, one time.

Let the priest again say:
'Do you also believe in Christ Jesus, the Son of God, who came from the Father, who, pre-existing, is with the Father, who was born from the Virgin Mary through the Holy Spirit, who was crucified in the days of Pontius Pilate, and died, and rose on the third day alive from the dead, and ascended to heaven, and sits at the right hand of the Father, and will come to judge the living and the dead?'
And when he says, 'I believe,' let him baptize him a second time.

And again let him say,
'Do you also believe in the Holy Spirit in the holy church?'
And let him who is being baptized say, 'I believe,' and thus let him baptize him a third time.

Afterwards, when he comes up [out of the water], let him be anointed by the presbyter with that oil over which the thanksgiving was recited, [the presbyter] saying over him, 'I anoint you with oil in the name of Jesus Christ.

Then let women be anointed by the widows, who sit in front, the presbyter reciting over them.

(But these widows, in the baptism, let them receive them beneath a veil, while the bishop says the profession, and thus those who renounce them.)

---

turning toward the west ... turning toward the east] T inserts into the ApTrad rite a rite of renunciation, or *apotaxis*, and a rite of adhesion prior to baptism, or *syntaxis* which is typical of Syrian baptismal rites. Cf. Cyril, *myst. cat.* 1.9; Theodore of Mopsuestia, *hom. cat.* 13, CH 19. theatres] Not in ApTrad or CH. who came from the Father, who, preexisting, is with the Father] Cooper and Maclean note (p. 18) that this interpolation into the Creed is paralleled in the so-called 'Detailed Creed' ascribed to Apollinaris of Laodicea, but that this fact indicates nothing more than its currency in extreme anti-Arian circles. in the name of Jesus Christ] T preserves the ApTrad wording; CH has a trinitarian formula.

[1] Or: minister

[II.9.]

Thenceforward let them be together in the church. Let the bishop lay a hand upon them after the baptism, saying and invoking over them thus:

[Invocation of the Holy Spirit]

Lord God, you who through your beloved Son Jesus Christ filled your holy Apostles with [the] Holy Spirit, and through the Spirit permitted your blessed prophets to speak; you who deemed these your servants worthy to be esteemed worthy, by your Christ, of forgiveness of sins through the washing of rebirth, and you who purged out from them all the gloom of error and darkness of unbelief, make them worthy to be filled with your Holy Spirit, in your *philanthropia*, bestowing upon them your grace, that they may truly serve you according to your will, truly, O God, and that they may perform your commandments in holiness, and, doing always those things which are of your will, may they come to your eternal tabernacles. Through you and through your beloved Son Jesus Christ, through whom to you be glory and power, with the Holy Spirit, for ever and ever.

Similarly also as he pours out the oil, when he places a hand on his head let him say: Anointing, I anoint [you] in almighty God and in Christ Jesus and in the Holy Spirit, that you may be for him a labourer who has perfect faith, and [that you may be] a vessel pleasing to him.

And when he seals him on the forehead[1], let him give him the Peace and say, the Lord God of the humble[2] be with you. And let him who has been sealed reply: and with your spirit. And thus for each one separately.

[II.10.]

From that time let them pray together with all the people.

Let the offering be received from the deacon, and thus let the shepherd[3] give thanks. The bread is offered for a type of my body. Let the cup be mixed with wine, with wine mixed with water, for it typifies[4] the blood and the bath,[5] that the inner man (that is,[6] which is of the soul) may be deemed worthy of those

---

II.9=ApTrad 22 (Dix). The invocation echoes the **ApTrad** prayer. **washing of rebirth**] Titus 3.5. **Anointing**] the **T** formula is more developed than that in **ApTrad**, adding the material 'that ... pleasing to him,' which articulates typical **T** themes. **vessel**] I Thess. 4.4, II Tim. 2.21. **the Peace**] Both **T** and **CH** interpret the bishop's kiss which appears in **ApTrad** as the Pax. **Lord God of the humble**] a unique **T** addition to the **ApTrad** text.

II.10=ApTrad 23 (Dix). **T** omits the **ApTrad** references to the milk and honey used in the **ApTrad** rite. **Let them pray**] **T** omits the Pax found after the prayers in **ApTrad**.

---

[1] Lit., between the eyes
[2] Or; lowly
[3] I.e., the bishop
[4] Lit., it is the typification (or: signification) of
[5] **M** it [is] the typification of the blood and the water of the bath
[6] that is: **S** omits

things like them; that is, [those things of] the body also. Let all the people, such as previously mentioned, receive of[1] the eucharist which has been offered with an amen. Let the deacons hover over [the offering][2], as previously mentioned. Let him who gives [the eucharist] say, 'The body of Jesus Christ, Holy Spirit, for healing of soul and body.' Let the one who receives say amen.

He who spills from the cup collects a judgment for himself. Similarly [it shall be] for him who sees and keeps quiet and does not accuse him [who spills from the cap], whoever he is.

Let those who receive the offering be urged[3] by the priests to be diligent in doing good works, to love strangers, to labour to cultivate service, in fasting[4] and in all good works. And let them also be taught about the resurrection of bodies. Let no one know the word concerning the resurrection before he is baptized. For this is a new precept[5] which has a new name which only he who receives [baptism] knows.

A deacon does not give the offering to a presbyter. Let him open the *pinax* (or paten),[6] and the presbyter takes [from it].

Let the deacon give [the eucharist] to the people by his hand.

When a presbyter is not present, a deacon may, of necessity, baptize.[7]

He who spills] echoes **ApTrad** 38 (Dix 32.3,4). **Let them also be taught**] echoes ApTrad 21. **A deacon does not give**]=ApTrad 22 (Dix 24).

[1] Lit., from
[2] Or: wave (fans) [over the offering]
[3] Or: exhorted
[4] Lit., in a fast
[5] Or: decree
[6] SYN: *pinax* and paten
[7] When ... baptize: **B** omits

3. Daily Prayer (I.22, 26, 32, 42, 43; II.24)

The *Testamentum* contains descriptions of daily prayer services, texts of daily prayers, and instructions concrning times of prayer. Some of this material derives from a version of **ApTrad** (II.24); however, the majority of **T** references to daily prayer practice derive from another source, perhaps the practice of the compiler's community.

The times **T** prescribes for daily prayer bear a resemblance to the hours of prayer found in the fourth-century 'urban monastic' traditions of Palestine and Cappadocia. However, **T** describes hours of private prayer, or prayer in private with a few others: essentially, the pre-Nicene practice of daily prayer. The closest parallels to the private or semi-private prayer practices of **T** appear in the Cappadocian treatise *De virginitate* (see Bib. No. 47), written in the last quarter of the fourth century.

T prescribes daily prayer for the bishop, widows, presbyters, and 'those of the people who are more perfect' (I.32), plus a daily gathering of the clergy and people at early dawn (I.26). Thus it seems that while **T** may describe the daily prayer of all the faithful, its prescriptions primarily concern a small group within a larger community. This picture clearly belongs to a post-Constantinian age, perhaps the last quarter of the fourth century.

A. TIMES OF PRAYER

Below is a table of the *Testamentum* references to times of prayer organized according to the times of prayer which appear in the *Testamentum*, the location of the references to times of prayer, and the persons for whom the document prescribes each hour.

	Bishop		Presyters		Widows		Deacons	Laypeople		Perfectiores
	I.22	I.26	I.26	I.32	I.42	I.43	I.26	I.26	II.24	I.32
early dawn	X	X	X				X	X	X	
dawn					X	X			X	
morning	X									
3rd hour	X								X	
6th hour	X								X	
9th hour	X								X	
12th/lamps	X									
evening									X	
1st of evening	X									
midnight	X^a			X^a	X^b				X^b	X^a
Pascha					X					
Epiphany					X					
Pentecost					X					

a Syriac: *mes'at-lelva*, 'middle of the night': perhaps not midnight, but a general time of prayer late at night
b Syriac: *pelgeh d-lelva* 'midnight'

[I. 26.]

At early dawn let the bishop gather the people together, so that the service is finished[1] at[2] the rising of the sun.

As the bishop says the first hymn of praise of dawn, with the presbyters and deacons and the others (the faithful also) [standing] nearby, let him say thus:

[Dawn Hymn of Praise.]

Let the priest say: Praise the Lord.

And let the people say: [It is] meet and right.

It is meet and right to praise, laud, and thank you who made all things, ineffable God. Stretching forth our souls upward, we raise a morning hymn of praise to you, Lord, you who are all-wise, powerful, greatly-loving God, strengthener and raiser-up of our souls, we praise you, Word who was begotten from the Father before the worlds, and who rests alone with your saints; you who are praised with the praises of archangels, you, the Creator uncreated by hands, the Revealer of invisible things, pure and spotless, you who have made known to us hidden mysteries of wisdom, and promised us immortal light, we lift up praise to you in pure holiness, we your servants, Lord.

And let the people say: We praise you, we bless you, we thank you, Lord, and we beseech you, our God.

O God, begetter of light, principle of life, giver of knowledge, gift of grace, maker of souls, and [who] makes beautiful [things], giver of the Holy Spirit, treasure of wisdom, and [who] does good things,

Lord, teacher of holiness, who sustains the worlds by his will, receiver of pure prayers, we praise you, only-begotten Son, first-born and Word of the Father, you who bestowed all your grace upon us who call you Helper, and [we praise] the Father, your Begetter. You who have an essence that cannot be harmed, where neither worm nor moth corrupts, who gives to those who trust you with

---

I.26 = unique to T. The opening two rubrics of this chapter may echo ApTrad 39 (Dix 33), which describes a gathering of the deacons, priests and the bishop for instruction. **ApTrad** gives no time for this gathering. The identity of the synaxis described in I.26ff. is unclear. Arranz quotes the Russian scholar Skaballanovich who believes that I.26-28 comprise 'a festive office,' while the prayers of I.32 describes the daily morning office. See Bibliography, No. 20. **early dawn]** T defines early dawn as 'when the morning star rises' (I.19), a time perhaps to be identified with the *orthros bathus* of Lk 24.1. **Dawn Hymn]** The text of this prayer appears in the Ethiopic *Me'erāf*, or book containing the common of the daily office, as the private presbyteral prayer known as the *kidān za-manfaqa lēlit*, or 'testament of midnight.' See Velat, 170-172. **O God, begetter of light]** This prayer appears in the Greek Liturgy of St. Mark as a prayer introducing the Lord's prayer following the anaphora (LEW 135.11-29), and also in the Coptic Liturgy of St. Basil (Renaudot I.20).

---

[1] Lit., be completed
[2] Or: until

their whole heart those things which angels yearned to behold; the guardian of eternal light and incorruptible treasures, you who enlightened the darkness within us by the will of your Father, you who lifted us up from the abyss to light, you who gave us life from death, you who bestowed upon us freedom from servitude, you who by the Cross have associated us with your Father, you who have led us to the heights of heaven through your Gospel, and you have comforted us through your prophets, you who associated us with God, the Father of lights, through your *qnōmā*.

Grant us, Lord, that we may praise you, our God, that we may always speak praises to you in unceasing thanksgiving, we your servants, Lord.

People: We praise you, we bless you, we give you thanks, we beseech you, our God.

Let the bishop say next:

We treble this hymn of praise from our mouths to you, as an image of your kingdom, O Son of God, who [are] through eternity, who [are] above all, with the Father, whom all creation praises, trembling from fear of your Spirit, from whom all nature fears, trembling, and every soul of the righteous blesses, with whom we all have taken refuge, who has calmed tumult, storms, [and] wind from us, [you] who [have] been a harbour of rests for us, and a refuge from corruption; in whom we have hope of eternal salvation; you who creates the tranquillity of clear skies for those at sea and buffeted by storm; you who are prayed to by those who are sick, and freely you heal; you who accompanies those confined in prison; you who have freed us from the bonds of death; who is the comforter of the poor and those who mourn, and of those who have laboured and have been made weary in the Cross; who turns back every threat from us, who have for our sake reproved the guile of Satan, you who drives out his threats and gives us courage, who thrusts out all error from those who trust in you, whom the prophets and apostles secretly praised;

We praise you, Lord, we lift up a doxology to you that, having understanding through you, we might rest in the habitations of life, as we do your will always. And grant us, Lord, to walk according to your commandments, and shepherd us all in mercy, both the small and the great, the prince and his people, the shepherd and his flock, for you, Lord, are our God, and blessed and praised is your Kingdom, of the Father, and of the Son, and of the Holy Spirit, both from before the worlds, and now and always, and to the ages of ages, and to unending worlds of the world. People: Amen.

Let them sing four psalms and hymns of praise: one[1] by Moses and of Solomon and of the other prophets. The psalmists thus: little boys, two virgins[2], three deacons, three presbyters.

And then let the hymn of praise be said by the bishop, or by one of the presbyters. Let it be said thus: The grace of our Lord be with you all.

And let the people say: And with your spirit.

And let a priest say: Let us again praise our Lord.

And let the people say: Meetly and rightly.

---

[1] Masc., referring to the psalm. Codex **B**; fem., referring to the hymn of praise
[2] Masc.

Let a priest say: Let your hearts be fixed.
And let the people say: We have [them fixed] with the Lord.
[Hymn of Praise of the Seal[1]]
O Lord, Father, giver of light, Overseer of all spiritual power, sealer of everlasting light and director of life, creator of gladness and of immortality, you who made us remove material darkness, and have bestowed immaterial light upon us, you who loosened the bonds of disobedience, and crowned us with the faith which is yours, you who are not distant from your servants, but are always amongst them, you who do not turn your face from those who supplicate[2] you in labour and your fear; you who perceive all things before they are thought, and inquire into all things before they are thought, you who give what you will give before we ask you, you are well-disposed to listen to those who serve you with an undivided soul. O king of the chief lights, and of the heavenly attendants, you who are the hearer of the praise-singing archangels, and you are pleased with them: hear us, O Lord, we beseech you. Grant us that an unceasing voice may praise you with confidence, laud you, and lift up a doxology that, remaining with you and guided by light, we may continually praise you.
People: We praise you, we bless you, we confess you, O Lord, and we supplicate you, our God.
Priest: O Lord Jesus, hear us; O Holy One, you who are the voice of the mute and inarticulate, the support of paralytics, the enlightener of the blind, the guide of the lame, cleanser of lepers, healer of material fluxes, healer of the deaf, rebuker of death, and torturer of darkness, ray of light, lamp which never goes out, the uneclipsed sun, [not] resting, but always giving light among his holy ones; you who fixed for everything together the good shape of the cosmos, you who are the well-proportioned reason, you who shines forth clearly over all, you who are the saviour of humanity, and converter of souls, you who are the overseer of all things, as is fitting, you, maker of angels, the one who adorns all, the Intelligence of the Father, you who established the worlds in understanding and wisdom, and fixed [them] together, and were sent to us from your eternal Father; you who are the mind of the incomprehensible and ineffable Spirit, the indicator of invisible things, you are glorious, and Wonderful is your name. On this account we also your servants, O Lord, praise you.
People: We praise you, we bless you, we confess you, and we supplicate you, our God.
Priest: We treble to you, O holy Lord, this hymn of praise to you who gave us indissoluble faith in you, through which you made us to conquer the bonds of death; [we praise] you who created upright minds[3] for those who trust in you, so

---

hymn of praise of the seal] The Ethiopic precedes this prayer with a signation by the bishop. Is this signation part of the original text, or has the Ethiopic translator added the action to make sense of the prayer title? The text of this prayer also appears in the Me'erāf as the kidān za-naghe, or 'testament of the morning.' See Velat, 172-173.
Wonderful] Isa. 9.6.

[1] Or: conclusion
[2] those who supplicate; a feminine participle in Syriac
[3] Or: opinions

that they might be gods; [we praise] you who imparted to us through the Spirit [the ability] to tread underfoot all the power of him who opposes, that we might not release those things which are unreleased; but you made friendship with the Father for us through your mediation. Hear us, your servants, O Lord, whom we do not neglect to supplicate, you who by our supplication gave power against him who opposed [us]; whom we always entreat for the overthrow of the evil one:

Hear us, O eternal King; comfort the widows, assist the orphans, [because] you have pity, purify those who are possessed by polluted spirits; make wise those who are unwise[1], turn back those who go astray, deliver those in prison; guard us all, for you, O Lord, are our God. Blessed and praised is your Kingdom. People: Amen.

[I.27.]

Afterwards, let the prayer be finished.[2] After this, let the reader read the prophets and the rest. Let a presbyter or deacon[3] read the Gospel. Afterwards, let the bishop or presbyter teach useful and profitable things. Then, let there be a prayer. Let the catechumens receive a laying-on of the hand.

[I.28.]

Then let the bishop teach the things of the mysteries to the people. If he is not present, a presbyter may say [the mysteries], so that the people know to whom they approach[4] and who is their God and Father.[5] Then let the teaching of the mysteries be said thus . . .

WIDOWS' PRAISE
[Extracts from I.42.]

Let her give praise by herself at fixed[6] times: at night, at dawn.

When she gives thanks or praises, if she has like-minded friends, virgins, it is well when they pray with her because of[7] the amen. But if not, [she should pray]

---

teaching of the mysteries] I.28, which follows this rubric, contains the so-called 'mystagogy,' which is a Christological confession containing an account of Christ's defeat of death during his descent to hell. The celebration of the eucharist follows the mystagogy. This text has a complex history, and shares many features with portions of the pseudo-Athanasian treatise *De virginitate*. See Bibliography No. 3.
I.42-43=unique to **T. like-minded friends**] This phrase, which **T** uses for the private prayer of both widows and the bishop (I.19), also appears in *De virg.* 10 (Von der Goltz, 43-44).

[1] **B**: unwise women
[2] Or: completed
[3] Or: minister; not the usual word for deacon
[4] Or: two whom they are offered
[5] Lit., who is God and Father to them
[6] Or: particular, special. Not the same word used in I.22 to describe the bishop's hours of prayer.
[7] Or: for the sake of

alone, and by herself both in the church and at home, especially at midnight.

The times in which it is fitting to give praise [are]: Saturday, Sunday, either Pascha or Epiphany or Pentecost. At the other times, let her be in humility, with psalms [and] hymns of praise [and] meditation.[1] Thus let her labour.

[I.43.]
[Night Praise of Widows.]

Holy, holy, without stain, you who dwell in light, O God of Abraham and Isaac and Jacob, God of Enoch and David, of Elijah and Elisha, of Moses, Joshua and of the prophets, of the others who in truth proclaimed your name, O God of the Apostles;

O God, you who have directed all by your thought,[2] and have blessed those who have lovingly put trust in you, my soul praises you with the strength of the spirit of my strength. My heart praises you, O Lord; [my heart praises] your might always. May all my strength praise you, O Lord, for if you wish, I am yours.

O God, God of the poor, because you are the helper of those who want, and [because] you look upon the humble and [are] the helper of the weak; assist me, O Lord, because by your grace you had pleasure in me to be your handmaid, because you bestowed a great name upon me, that I might be called a Christian. You who have set me free from servitude through my service to God, eternal mighty one, the seer of all, [assist me] so that I might praise you because I have not been found guilty. Yes, O Lord God, confirm my heart until it is perfected in Holy Spirit. Rejuvenate us for the building of your holy church.

Son and Word and Will of the Father, Christ who came for the salvation of the human race, who suffered and was buried and rose, you [who] again were glorified by him who sent you, turn, help, O Lord, direct your thoughts by the firm faith of the Spirit. Glorify your name in us, because in your Father and in you and in the Holy Spirit is our hope for ever and ever.

Let her say amen with those with her.

[Dawn Praise of Widows Who Sit in Front.]

You, eternal God, the guide of our souls, maker of light, treasure of life, you who are pleased with the praises and prayers of holy people, loving compassion, merciful, kind, King of all, and God our Lord, my spirit which sends unceasing cries to you, praises [you], for it is your handmaid who entreats you, Lord, that you might perfect in your handmaid the spirit of thought and piety and upright knowledge.

Enoch] Enoch appears also in the bishop's ordination prayer (cf. I.21). **Son and Word and Will]** note the Christological terminology in this prayer, as elsewhere in the T prayers (cf. I.32).

[1] Or: study
[2] **B**: thoughts

I praise you, Lord, you who attended to our poverty: [to] all [our] perturbance and agitation, wrath and all contention and evil habit; [I praise] him who prepared [and] changed the senses of my mind, that I might serve you alone, O God, you who adorned your holy Church with diverse ministries, you who drives out all doubt from your handmaid, [all] fear, weakness, and [who] holds the thoughts of those who serve you in uprightness.

I praise you, O God, you who enlightened me with the light of your knowledge, through your only-begotten Son our Lord Jesus Christ. Through whom to you be praise and might for ever and ever. Amen.
And let her say amen with those with her.

PRESBYTERS' DAILY PRAISE
[I.32.]
Let them [i.e., the presbyters] say a daily hymn of praise in the church, each of them at his [own] time, thus:
The grace of our Lord be with you all.
People: And with your spirit.
Priest: Praise the Lord.
People: It is meet and right.

[Daily Hymn of Praise.]

Priest: [We praise] you, O Father of incorruptibility, deliverer of our souls and confirmer of our thoughts and guard of our hearts, who enlightened our hearts and nullified the darkness of our mind through the knowledge which is in you, you who through the Cross of your only-begotten made the old man given over to corruption new again for incorruptibility, you who brought error to an end, and through your commandments has caused humankind to pass over to immortality, and sought the one who was lost, we servants, also the people, praise you.
People: We praise you, [etc.]
Priest: We praise you, Lord, whom the never-quiet doxologies of the praise-singing archangels and the praises of glories and the psalms of dominions continually praise, we praise you, O Lord, you who sent your Thought, your Word, your Wisdom, your Action, he who is at first, and was with you from before the worlds, the uncreated Word of the Uncreated, but [who] appeared incarnate at the end of times for the salvation of created humanity, your beloved Son Jesus Christ, he who set us free from the servitude of slavery. On this account, as we are accustomed to being your servants, [we], O Lord, also the people, praise you.
People: We praise you, [etc.]

I.32 = unique to T. The text of this prayer (minus the rubrics) is also known in Ethiopic as the *kidān-za-sark*, or private presbyteral prayer to be said at night (Velat, 174). The *kidān* is found in a larger collection of Ethiopic prayers known as the *me'erāf* (Bibliography No. 14). **with you from before the worlds]** similar to a phrase in the baptismal creed (II.8). **uncreated Word of the Uncreated]** strong anti-Arian phrase typical of T.

Priest: To you we treble praise from our hearts, O lifegiving Lord who care for the souls of the poor and do not neglect the spirits of those who are afflicted, the assister of those who are persecuted, the helper of those who are buffeted at sea, the deliverer of those who are afflicted, the nurturer[1] of the hungry, the avenger of those who suffer wrong, lover of the faithful, the intimate acquaintance of the holy, the habitation of the pure, dwelling-place of those who call out to you in truth, the protector of widows, the deliverer of orphans, you who give right guidance[2] to your church and who planted love-feasts, ministries, hospitalities[3] of the faithful, participation in the Spirit, gifts of grace and miracles:

We praise you, we unceasingly depict in ourselves the image of your Kingdom for your sake, also [for the sake] of your beloved Son Jesus Christ, through whom to you be praise and might with the Holy Spirit, to the ages of ages, for ever and ever. Amen.

And let the people say amen.

If anyone speaks prophetic words, let him speak. He has a reward.

At midnight[4] let the sons of priestly service and those of the people who are more mature[5] give praise by themselves. For also in that hour our Lord praised his Father as he rose.

See, sons of light: he who believes the words of the Lord walks as he walked in this world, that he may be there even as he himself is.

[II.24.]

Always let the people be anxious for the early dawn, that rising and washing their hands they may immediately pray, and thus each one go to the work he wishes.

Let all be anxious to pray at the third hour, with mourning and labour, whether at the church or in the house because they cannot go [to the church]. For this is the hour of the fixing of the Only-begotten on the Cross.

But at the sixth hour likewise let there be prayer with sorrow, for then the day was divided by darkness. thus let there be a voice like to the prophets, and to the creation, mourning.

---

sons of priestly service] the presbyters, or all the clergy?

For also in that hour] The same tradition appears verbatim in *De virginitate* 20 (Von der Goltz, 55-56).

II.24 = ApTrad 41 (Dix 35, 36). Phillips has suggested that T has followed the general pattern of private prayer of ApTrad 35-38, but has expanded ApTrad 35 beginning with prayer at rising into a full horarium as found in ApTrad 41; see L. Edward Phillips 'Daily Prayer in the *Apostolic Tradition* of Hippolytus' in JTS N.S. 40.2 (October 1989) 389-400. rising] T has made the ApTrad prescription of rising for instruction into an early dawn (same time as I.26) hour of prayer.

[1] Or: guardian
[2] Or: direction
[3] Or: receptions
[4] Or: In the middle of the night
[5] Or: perfect

But also at the ninth hour let the prayer be prolonged as with a hymn of praise like [that of] the souls of those who praise God who does not lie, who has remembered his holy ones, and has sent his Word and Wisdom to enlighten them. For at this hour life was opened to believers, and blood and water poured out from our Lords side.

But at evening, when it is the beginning of another day, he has caused us to give praise, showing an image[1] of the Resurrection .

But at midnight, let them rise in a praising and lauding fashion because of the Resurrection.

At dawn, [let them rise] in a praising manner with psalms, because after he rose he praised the Father while they were singing psalms.

---

ninth hour] T makes two hours out of the **ApTrad** prescription: ninth hour and evening. I.19 refers to the bishop's prayer at the twelfth hour or lamplighting. Is evening the same time? T also omits the **ApTrad** bedtime hour of prayer. **midnight]** is the prescription to rise 'in a praising and lauding fashion' an echo of the tradition concerning midnight prayer found in I.30? **dawn]** Canons of Basil 29 (Riedel, KRQ 246) associates the hour of cockcrow (earlier than the hour of dawn) with the Resurrection. **while they were singing psalms]** the tradition behind this prescription is unknown. Cf. Ps. 21.23 (LXX).

[1] Gk *eikon*

4. Ordination (I.21, 30, 38, 41, 44, 45)

The *Testamentum* contains ordination prayers for bishops (I.21), presbyters (I.30), deacons (I.38), widows (I.41), readers (I.45), and subdeacons (I.44). **ApTrad** serves as the primary source in the bishop's and deacon's prayers. In general, **T** expands the **ApTrad** prayers with large, discrete blocks of material easily distinguishable from the **ApTrad** material surrounding it. Particularly interesting is the document's use of the same term for the ordination of widows as it uses for the ordination of bishops and presbyters (see Notes).

[I.21.]
Let him who is of this sort receive laying on of hands on the first day of the week, all consenting to his appointment and bearing witness to him, [along] with all the neighbouring presbyters and bishops. Let those bishops lay hands on him, first having washed their hands. But let the presbyters stand near them quietly, with awe, lifting up their hearts in silence. Next, [let] the bishops lay hands on him, saying:

We lay hands on this servant of God who has been chosen by the Spirit for the firm and pious establishment of the monarchic and indissoluble church of the invisible and Living God, and for the preservation of true judgment [1]and divine and[2] holy revelations, and of divine gifts and trustworthy doctrines of the Trinity; through the cross, through the resurrection, through incorruptibility[3], in the holy Church of God.

After this, let one of the bishops charged by the other bishops lay hands on him, saying the invocation of the ordination thus:

PRAYER OF THE *CHEIROTONIA*[4] OF A BISHOP
O God, you who have made and fixed all things in power, and have founded the inhabited world in thought, you who have adorned the crown of all these things made by you, who have granted these to keep your commandments in fear; you who have bestowed understanding of truth upon us, and have made us to know your good Spirit; you who sent your beloved Son, the only begotten Saviour without stain, for our salvation;

O God and Father of our Lord Jesus Christ, Father of mercies and God of all comfort, [you] who everlastingly dwell in the pure heights, who are exalted, glorious, revered, great, and all-seeing, who know all things[5] before they are, with whom all things were before they came into existence; you who gave

----

I.21 = ApTrad 2.

[1] SYN: judgments
[2] SYN: omits divine and
[3] SYN: through the resurrection of incorruptibility
[4] Gk transliterated
[5] all things: SYN reads: their mind

enlightenment to the church[1] through the grace of your only begotten Son; you who predetermined from the beginning [that] those who take pleasure in just things and do those things which are holy [should] dwell in your mansions; you who chose Abraham who pleased you through his faith, and who translated holy Enoch to the treasury of life; who ordered princes and priests for your high sanctuary, Lord, who called [them] to praise and glorify your name and [the name] of your only-begotten in the place of your glory:

Lord God, you who did not leave your high sanctuary without a ministry before the foundations of the world, and even before the foundations of the world you adorned and beautified your sanctuaries with faithful princes and priests in a type of your heaven; you, Lord, even now have been pleased to be praised, and have deigned that there be leaders for your people.

Make shine and pour out understanding and grace from your princely Spirit which you delivered to your beloved Son Jesus Christ; give, O God, wisdom, reasoning, strength, power, unity of spirit to do all things by your operation.

Give your Spirit, O holy God, who was given to your Holy One; send [him] to your holy and pure Church and to every place which has been consecrated to you[2]; and grant, O Lord, that this your servant may be pleasing to you for doxology[3] and unceasing praise, O God; for fitting hymns, suitable times, acceptable prayers, faithful petitions, correct doctrine, a humble heart, conduct of life, and humility and truth, for the knowledge of uprightness.

O Father who knows hearts, [grant] to this servant whom you have chosen for the episcopate to feed your holy flock, and to stand in the high-priesthood without blame, serving you day and night.[4] Grant[5] that your countenance may appear to him; make him worthy, O Lord, to offer you the offerings of your holy Church circumspectly, with all awe. Grant him to have your powerful Spirit to loose all bonds, just as you granted to your Apostles. In order [that he might] please you in humility, fill him with love, knowledge, understanding, discipline, maturity, strength, and a pure heart, as he prays for the people and while he mourns for those who act foolishly[6] and draws them toward relief, while he offers you praise and thanksgiving and prayers for a sweet savour. Through your beloved Son our Lord Jesus Christ, through whom to you be praise and honour and might, with the Holy Spirit, both before the worlds[7], and now and always and to the generation of generations and to worlds without end of worlds. Amen.

Let the people say, Amen.

Then let them cry out, He is worthy, he is worthy, he is worthy.

After he is [ordained], let the people keep feast for three days as a sign of him who rose from the dead in three days. Then let everyone give him the Peace.

---

your princely Spirit] T omits the **ApTrad** reference to the Spirit given to the Apostles.

[1] to the church: SYN omits
[2] which ... to you: SYN: which is your sanctuary
[3] calque for Gk *doxologia*
[4] The preceding sentence contains no verb in the Syriac
[5] SYN: and grant
[6] SYN: those who suffer
[7] both ... worlds: SYN omits

[I.30.]

Then let the ordination of a presbyter be thus: after all the priestly *qyāmā* have brought him, while the bishop lays his hand on his head and the presbyters are touching him and holding him, let the bishop begin, saying thus:

PRAYER OF THE *CHEIROTONIA*[1] OF A PRESBYTER

O God, Father of our Lord Jesus Christ, the Ineffable, the Luminary, who has neither beginning nor end, Lord, you who have ordered all things, and set [them] in a limit, and in thought have determined the order for all things you have created:

hear us, and turn toward this your servant, and make [him] a partaker and grant him the spirit of grace and of reason and of strength, [the] spirit of the presbyterate[2] which does not age, indissoluble, homogeneous,[3] loving the faithful, admonishing, [in order] to help and govern your people in labour, in fear, with a pure heart, in holiness, and in excellency, and in wisdom, and by the operation of your Holy Spirit through your care, Lord.

In like manner as when you attended to your chosen people, you commanded Moses to ask for the elders[4], when you filled [them with] Holy Spirit you bestowed your minister[5]; and now, O Lord, bestow[6] your unfailing Spirit upon him, which you gave to those who became disciples through you and to all those who through them truly believed in you; and make him worthy, (being filled with your wisdom and with your hidden mysteries) to shepherd your people in the holiness of a pure and true heart, praising, blessing, lauding, acknowledging, always offering a doxology, day and night, to your holy and glorious name, labouring in cheerfulness and patience, so that he might be an instrument of your Holy Spirit, always having and bearing the cross of your only-begotten Son, our Lord Jesus Christ, through whom to you be glory and might, with the Holy Spirit, to all the ages of ages.

Let the people say, Amen.

Let them give him the Peace, both priests and people, with a holy kiss.

I.30 = ApTrad 7 (Dix 6). T adds to the **ApTrad** prayer phrases describing the work of the presbyter typical of other passages in the document (cf. I.32), with its emphasis upon holiness, the operation of the Holy Spirit, labour, and the presbyter's work of prayer.

[1] Gk transliterated
[2] some Ethiopic MSS read 'spirit of holiness'
[3] calque of Gk *homogenes*
[4] SYN: an elder
[5] The Syriac is unclear. The Ethiopic reads: 'Comme tu as voulu que par ton peuple il soit élu, selon le commandment que tu as donne a Moise d'interroger les anciens, et tu les as rassaisiés de ton Ésprit que tu as donné a ton serviteur Moise.'
[6] **M**: you have bestowed.

[I.38.]

Then let the ordination of a deacon be thus: let the bishop alone lay his hand[1] on him, because he is ordained not to the priesthood but to the ministry of attending to the bishop and the Church. Therefore, let the bishop say thus over the deacon:

PRAYER OF THE *CHEIROTONIA*[2] OF A DEACON

O God, you who created all things, and who adorned [them] by the Word, you who rest in the pure ages, you who ministered eternal life to us through your prophets, you who have enlightened us with the light of your knowledge;

O God who do great things, the maker of all glory, the Father of our Lord Jesus Christ, whom you sent to minister to your will so that all the human race might be saved; you[3] made known to us and revealed your Thought, your Wisdom, your Action, your beloved Son Jesus Christ, the Lord of light[4], the Prince of princes, and God of gods:

Bestow[5] the spirit of grace and diligence upon this your servant, so that there might be given to him diligence, serenity, strength, [and] power to please you. Grant him, O Lord, to be a lawful labourer without shame, kind, a lover of orphans, a lover of the pious, a lover of widows[6], fervent in spirit, a lover of good things.[7]

Enlighten[8], Lord, the one you have loved and have appointed to minister to your Church to offer in holiness to your sanctuary[9] those things offered to you from the inheritance of your high-priesthood, so that he may minister without blame and in purity and holiness, and with a pure conscience may [he] be proved worthy of this high and exalted rank through your will, praising you continuously through your only-begotten Son Jesus Christ our Lord, through whom be praise and might to you for ever and ever. The people: Amen.

[I.41.]

Let her ordination be thus: while she is praying at the entrance[10] of the altar and looking down, let the bishop say in a low voice so that [only] the priests can hear:

I.38 = ApTrad 8 (Dix 9). **T** has retained the **ApTrad** prayer, adding a few phrases describing the nature of God and the Son, plus an expansion of the description of the deacon's duties.

I.41 = unique to **T**. **ApTrad** 10 (Dix 11) says explicitly that widows are to be appointed rather than ordained. **T**, however, applies the same word for 'ordination' (Syriac *mettasthānuta*) to widows as it does to the bishop, presbyter, deacon, and subdeacon, another indicator of the high regard in which **T** places the widows of the community.

[1] **S**: hands
[2] Gk transliterated
[3] you . . . Jesus Christ: ETH: tu vous as revele ta volonte et la puissance et ta sagesse et la providence
[4] SYN: lights
[5] Lit., give
[6] SYN: chaste widows
[7] fervent . . . things: SYN omits
[8] **M**: you have enlightened; SYN has no verb here
[9] to your sanctuary: SYN omits
[10] **B**: at the east

O God, holy one and exalted one, who sees humble women, who has chosen the weak and the mighty, O honoured one, who has created[1] even those things which are despised: bestow, O Lord, a spirit of power upon this your handmaid, and strengthen her with your truth, that, keeping your commandment and labouring in your sanctuary, she may become an honoured vessel for you and may [give] praise on the day[2] on which you will praise your poor ones, O Lord.

And[3] grant her the power gladly to practise these your teachings which you fixed as a rule for your handmaid. Give her, O Lord, a spirit of humility and of power and patience and of kindness, that, bearing your burden with ineffable joy, she may endure labours.

Yes, O Lord God, you who know our weakness, perfect your handmaid for the praise of your house; strengthen her for edification and a good example; sanctify, [her] grant wisdom, encourage [her], O God, because your kingdom is blessed and glorious, O God [and] Father. And to you be praise, and to your only-begotten Son our Lord Jesus Christ and to the Holy Spirit[4] [who is] honourable and worshipped and life-giving[5] and consubstantial[6] with you, now and before all worlds and to the generation of generations and to the ages of ages. The people: Amen.

[I.44. Concerning Subdeacons]

Likewise let the subdeacon be ordained[7]; let him bow while the bishop prays over him. On Sunday let the bishop say over him[8], all the people listening:

N., serve and obey the gospel in the fear of God. In holiness cultivate self-knowledge; observe purity; practice the ascetic life; regard and obey and listen in humility; do not neglect prayers and[9] fasts, that the Lord may grant you rest and deem you worthy of a greater rank.

And let all the priests say, So be it, so be it, so be it.

---

rule] Syriac qānonā. T uses this word in a number of places to describe its prescriptions (I.19, I.45) **life-giving ... consubstantial**] The Ethiopic lacks this technical theological terminology which came into general use only shortly before the Council of Constantinople in A.D. 381. The Ethiopic doxology reads: Gloire au Père, au Fils et a l'Esprit Saint, maintenant et toujours et pour les siècles des siècles, amen. Rahmani comments concerning *homoousios* in the text: *Videtur haec vox a manu recentiori introducta* (99).
I.44 = ApTrad 13 (Dix 14).

[1] **B**: has called
[2] **M**: in (or: with) the name
[3] **B** omits
[4] **B**: your Spirit
[5] calque of Gk *zoopoios*
[6] calque of Gk *homoousios*
[7] SYN: and the subdeacon is ordained; let him bow ...
[8] SYN: to him
[9] SYN: omits

[I.45. Concerning the Reader]

The reader is constituted pure, gentle, humble,[1] well-tested, skilled and[2] learned, mindful, vigilant, that he may be suitable for a higher rank. First let the book be given to him while the people look on, on the first day of the week. A hand is not laid upon him, but he hears from the bishop:

N., Christ has called you[3] to be a minister of his words; take care and strive, that you may appear approved[4] both in this rule and[5] in a higher rank, even to Jesus Christ,[6] that he[7] may reward you for these things with a good wage in his eternal mansions.[8]

And let the priests say, So be it, so be it, so be it.

I.45 = ApTrad 11 (Dix 12).

[1] **D**: omits
[2] SYN omits
[3] SYN: whom Christ has blessed
[4] SYN adds: at the last
[5] both . . . and: SYN has a lacuna here
[6] even . . . Christ: SYN omits
[7] SYN: Christ
[8] in . . . mansions: SYN omits

5. Architecture (I.19)

The *Testamentum* provides a full description of a church building, which has affinities with Syrian church structures of the fourth century. The most recent work on church architecture in the *Testamentum* is P. Post's 1981 article 'La liturgie en tant qu'architecture? Remarques sur la relation entre le *"Testamentum Domini Jesu Christi"* et l'architecture des églises dans l'Illyricum oriental' in *Bijdragen* 42 (1981), 392-420.

[I.19.]

I shall tell you how the sanctuary[1] ought to be; then I shall explain the holy rule of the priests of the church.

Let the church be as follows: let it have three entrances for a type of the Trinity.

Let there be a house for the deacons[2] from the right of the right-hand entrance, so that the eucharists, or offerings which are offered, may be visible.[3] Let the atrium[4] have a stoa all around, to the house of the deacons.

Within, then, the front court let there be a *baptisterion*[5] twenty-one cubits in length, for a type of the complete number of the prophets. Let the breadth [be] twelve cubits for a type of those who have been foredetermined to proclaim the Gospel. [Let there be] one entrance, three exits.

Let the church have a house for the catechumens. Let the same also be a house for the exorcists. It should not be separate from the church, but such that as they enter[6] and are in it[7] they may hear the readings and[8] spiritual hymns of praise, and the psalms.

Then[9] let there be a throne at the east.[10] On the right and the left [let there be] places for the presbyters, so that those who are more exalted and honoured sit on the right, and those who labour in[11] the word; those who are middle-aged [sit] in the area to the left [of the throne].

I.19 = unique to **T. offerings . . . may be visible**] Taft, *Great Entrance* 19, suggests that **T** here provides evidence that the faithful deposited their breads for the eucharist with the deacon before the liturgy, not in an offertory procession.

[1] Lit., house of holiness
[2] Lit., house of the deacons
[3] Lit., seen
[4] Lit., front court
[5] Lit., house for the place of baptism
[6] **M** reads: but as they enter
[7] The text as printed contains a masculine pronoun, but the sentence requires the feminine.
[8] and: **M** omits
[9] Lit., afterwards
[10] Rahmani cn: **M, B** read 'altar'
[11] Or: with

Let the place of the throne be[1] raised by three steps, for it is right that the altar be there.

Let the house have two stoas, on the right and on the left, for the men and the women.

Let all places be lighted, for a type and for the readings.

Let the altar have a veil of pure linen, because he is without stain.

Similarly also the house of baptism: let it be under a veil.

Let a place be built for recording [names], so that when a priest and chief deacon sits with the readers, he may write the names of those who offer offerings or [the names] of those on behalf of whom they have offered, that when the holy things are offered by the bishop, the reader or chief deacon may name them in the memorial[2] which the priests[3] and people offer on their behalf, in[4] intercession. For this is a type also in heaven.

Let the place of the presbyters be within the veil, near the place of recording.

Let the *chorbanas* and *gazophylakion*[5] be near the house of the deacons.

Let the place of reading be a little removed[6] from the altar.

Let the bishop's house be near the place called the atrium.[7]

Also again [let there be a house] of the widows who are called 'those who sit in front.'[8]

Also again [let there be a house] of the presbyters and deacons; let it be behind the house of baptism.

Let the deaconesses remain near the door of the Lord's house.

Let the church have a house of hospitality near by, so that the chief deacon may receive strangers.

---

veil] cf. Lev. 16.2; 21, 23. **CH** 29 and 36 also refer to the veil of the altar. **chorbanas and gazophylakion**] cf. Matt. 27.6, Mark 12.41

[1] The verb here is masculine (referring to the throne), when it should be feminine (in reference to the place of the throne).
[2] Or: commemoration
[3] Codex **B** reads: a (or: the) priest
[4] Or: with
[5] So R translates the Syriac. Or: treasury and contribution box.
[6] SYN: beyond
[7] Lit., front court
[8] Gk *prokathemenai*

6. Liturgical Year (II.12, 18, 19, 20)

The liturgical year in T is primitive. Besides the 'first day', Sabbath (i.e., Saturday) and fast days, T mentions only Pascha (always a transliteration from the Greek), Epiphany and Pentecost. These three feasts have special importance for the prayer which is the responsibility of the widows of the community (I.42). In addition, the liturgical calendar appears to regulate the teaching functions of the T community to some extent (see I.28).

The simplicity of the T calendar is striking when compared with the cycle of feasts found in the Apostolic Constitutions, which dates from 375-380. Particularly notable is the lack of the feast of Christmas in T. It is well-known that Christmas was a relative latecomer to the liturgical calendars of the Eastern churches. However, the lack of the feast of Christ's nativity in T does not necessarily mean that T was compiled earlier than AC (although that possibility is not ruled out). The *Testamentum* may have been written in a part of the Roman Empire in which the feast of Christmas did not find a place in the liturgical calendar until very late.

T also provides information on the feast of Pascha. It describes very short, two-day fast before the feast. The document does not describe a lengthy fast before Easter, nor does it indicate the development of the last week before Pascha into a Holy Week of individual commemorations.

Below is a collection of T prescriptions for the Paschal celebration. For a detailed commentary on II.18-20, see Quasten, Bib. No. 39.
Saturday: I.22, 23, 28
Sunday: I. 21, 22, 23, 28
Pascha: I.28, II.6, 7, 18-20
Paschal fast:
  Thursday: II.6, 8, 11
  Friday and Saturday: II.6, 8, 12
Forty days of Pascha: II.8
Epiphany: I.28, 42
Pentecost: I.28, 42; II.12

[II.12.]
Let the conclusion[1] of Pascha be at midnight, after the Saturday.
At Pentecost no one may fast or kneel, for they are days of rest and joy.
Let those who bear burdens of labour refresh themselves a little the days[2] of Pentecost, and each Sunday.

II.12 = unique to T.

[1] Lit., loosing
[2] Codex B reads: in the days

Before the oblation of the offering, let the bishop speak aptly for the offering[1], while those dressed in white receive from each other and say hallelujah.

[II.18.]

In the days of Pascha[2], especially the last [days], on the Friday and Saturday, let there be prayers night and day according to the number of hymns of praise. Let the full word be interpreted, and [let] the readings be diverse and frequent.[3] Let the vigils and the night anticipations be in good order.[4]

[II.19.]

Concerning the deacons who walk and work among the women, lest the children are disorderly: let the readers assist; similarly also the subdeacons. Let them not allow them to slumber, for that night is an image of the Kingdom, especially that of the Saturday. Let those who labour and are weary be weary until midnight.[5] Let the catechumens first be dismissed, receiving blessings[6] from the broken bread.

When the faithful are dismissed with order[7] and understanding[8], let them go to their houses. In their meals[9] let them not forget the prayers.

Let the priests not interrupt their ministries.

Let the women go, each one accompanying her husband.

Let the widows remain in the temple until dawn, because they have food there.

Let the female virgins likewise stay in the temple, and let the bishop assist and take care of them. And let the deacons minister to them.[10]

Let the presbyters remain near the bishop until dawn, praying and resting. Similarly for the newly-baptized.

Let female virgins ready for marriage accompany their mothers. Thus let them go. This is thus fitting.

---

those dressed in white] CH 37 refers to presbyters dressed in white.
II.18 = unique to T. The Synodicon contains two versions of this chapter (pp. 59, 60). The first reads 'night anticipations,' the other reads 'night stations'.
II.19 = unique to T. CH 38, which also discusses the Paschal night, contains a prescription that no one is to sleep until the morning.

[1] Or: what is fitting for the offering
[2] Gk *pascha* transliterated
[3] Or: continuous, often
[4] Translation of Gk *eustathēs*
[5] **M**: until its midst
[6] **B**: a blessing
[7] **B**: with their ranks
[8] Or: knowledge
[9] **B**: in the meal
[10] **B**: them (masc.)

[II.20.]

Let the bishop command that they proclaim that no one taste anything until the offering is finished.[1] And let the entire body of the church receive new nourishment.

Then after the evening let the baptizands be baptized after one reading.

If someone eats something other [than the eucharist] before receiving and partaking of the eucharist, he sins and his fast is not reckoned to him.

When the catechumens are dismissed, let a hand be laid upon them.

If one of the faithful stays [at home] because of sickness, let a deacon take him [or: bring him] the offering.

If one is a presbyter who cannot come [to church], let a presbyter take [the offering] to him.

Similarly [for] a woman, if she is pregnant[2] she is sick and is not able to fast these two days, let her fast that one day[3], taking on that [day] first bread and water, and if she is unable to come [to church], let a deaconess take [the offering] to her.

II.20 = unique to **T**. **after the evening]** perhaps a reference to baptism after vespers (cf. II.18).

[1] Or: completed
[2] **S**: if a pregnant woman
[3] M,B: let them fast one